The Institute of Biology's Studies in Biology, no. 130

Evolution and Pollution

A. D. Bradshaw

Ph.D., F. I. Biol.
Professor of Botany,
University of Liverpool

T. McNeilly

Ph.D.
Lecturer in Botany,
University of Liverpool

Edward Arnold

First published in 1981
by Edward Arnold (Publishers) Limited
41 Bedford Square, London WC1 3DQ

British Library Cataloguing in Publication Data
Bradshaw, A D
Evolution and pollution. – (Institute of Biology. Studies in biology; no. 130
ISSN 0537–9024).
1. Evolution 2. Pollution
I. Title II. McNeilly, T III. Series
575 QH371.

ISBN 0–7131–2818–6

Photo Typeset by Macmillan India Ltd. Bangalore

Printed and bound in Great Britain
at The Camelot Press Ltd, Southampton

General Preface to the Series

Because it is no longer possible for one textbook to cover the whole field of biology while remaining sufficiently up to date, the Institute of Biology proposed this series so that teachers and students can learn about significant developments. The enthusiastic acceptance of 'Studies in Biology' shows that the books are providing authoritative views of biological topics.

The features of the series include the attention given to methods, the selected list of books for further reading and, wherever possible, suggestions for practical work.

Readers' comments will be welcomed by the Education Officer of the Institute.

1981

Institute of Biology
41 Queen's Gate
London SW7 5HU

Preface

Pollution is, unfortunately, an inevitable part of our world. At its worst it can have very severe effects: plants and animals are progressively stressed and finally eliminated. But ecosystems and species do have a considerable resilience. This book discusses the remarkable resilience in species which can be provided by evolution. Natural selection can cause substantial genetic changes in populations which allow species to tolerate high levels of pollution. This is of interest not only to people concerned with pollution but also to everyone interested in the mechanism of evolution, because some of the best examples of evolution in action now available to us, are of evolution in relation to pollution.

This book looks at the evolution that occurs in plants growing on sites contaminated with metals, influenced by air pollutants, and even treated with herbicides. We find that evolution can be very rapid and exciting. The same is being found in animals. We have chosen not to use the word 'plants' in our title because the remarkable examples that we discuss are of importance and relevance to everyone, whether they are interested in plants, animals, or micro-organisms.

Liverpool, 1981

A.D.B.
T.McN.

Contents

1 Variation and Selection

1.1 Evolution and pollution

Pollution is a problem that is as old as civilization. The first chimneys and the first metal mines were as much sources of polluting substances as the more gigantic sources we think of today, when we are each responsible every year for about three-quarters of a tonne of pollutants going into the air alone. The damage caused by pollution was recognized a long time ago. In 1650 John Evelyn recorded in his diary 'the hellish and dismal cloud of sea-coale' over London so that 'catarrhs, phthisicks, coughs and consumptions rage more in this one City than in the whole Earth besides', and in 1727 John Fairchild wrote a book *The City Gardener* in which he described the plants which could not be grown in London because of the smoke.

But all these and later writers recorded only the deleterious effects of pollution, damage to trees, disappearance of species and barrenness of polluted areas. They thought of the effects of pollution on living organisms only as a downhill process, resulting in progressively greater damage, in which first one organism and then another succumbed to its effects. To a large extent the ability of individual species to hold out against pollution has been seen as something determined by the inherent characteristics of the species. Thus it seems natural that evergreen conifers such as the Scots pine (*Pinus sylvestris*) should be more susceptible to air pollutants than deciduous tree species such as the London plane (*Platanus acerifolia*) because its leaves would be exposed to the higher levels of atmospheric pollution occurring in the winter. Other variations in susceptibility might not be so easy to explain, but they would, in one way or another, be thought of as being due to the inherent characteristics of the species.

Yet in 1934 an Austrian, PRAT, became puzzled when he found plants of red campion (*Silene dioica*) growing on the highly polluted wastes of a copper mine near Piesky in Austria, on which little else would grow, especially since it was a common plant in normal soils. He collected seed from plants on the mine as well as on ordinary soils, and grew them on soil mixed with different amounts of copper carbonate. In the space of a few weeks he was able to show that while seedlings produced from seed of the mine plants continued to thrive in soil mixed with copper carbonate, seedlings from the plants from normal soil did not, although both lots of seed grew well on normal soil (Fig. 1–1).

The paper is short, and Prat was content to record the differences

Fig. 1–1 The first indication that plant evolution could occur in polluted environments: growth of populations of red campion, I from a normal soil, II from a copper mine, on soil mixed with different amounts of copper carbonate (look particularly at the close up of I and II at the highest copper level) (PRAT, 1934).

between the two populations, and to suggest only briefly that they might be the outcome of natural selection. By this time the process of evolution was well understood and good evidence for the way in which it could cause local differences between populations within plant species had been described. But Prat had discovered an important extension of the principles of evolution: that evolutionary change could occur in man-made as well as natural environments. Like so many scientific discoveries, it was virtually ignored for thirty years. But it is the starting point of a great deal of work showing us just how the evolutionary mechanisms proposed by Charles Darwin operate in practice in plants.

1.2 The basis of evolution

Darwin's explanation for the way in which evolution occurs is very simple. His starting point was four observations, from which he made three crucial deductions:

Observation *i*) The numbers of all organisms tend to increase logarithmically.

Observation *ii*) Yet on the whole their numbers remain more or less constant.

deduction ∴ There must be a *struggle for existence* – some organisms survive and some die.

Observation *iii*) Organisms vary – some are better adapted to their environments than others.

deduction ∴ In the struggle for existence it will be these that tend to survive – there is *natural selection.*

Observation *iv*) Much of this variation is inherited.

deduction ∴ The results of natural selection will accumulate as one generation replaces another – there will be *evolutionary change.*

This remains the only explanation of evolution that is plausible today.

Darwin's main problem was that he had no direct observations to illustrate his deductions. It is surprising to realize that nowhere in the *Origin of Species* is there any example of natural selection in action. Nor is his evidence on the origin and inheritance of variation satisfactory. It required later work to demonstrate that characters are determined by genes which are passed on from one generation to another in a complex manner. The final surprise is that he gives no examples of evolution actually occurring naturally: he had to make do with the results of animal breeding, which had impressed him greatly.

We are now, one hundred years later, in a very different position. Not only do we understand the mechanisms of variation but we have excellent evidence for natural selection, and can show how the two interact to give evolution. This occurs so rapidly that we can observe it taking place.

Evolution has usually had time to bring species, and more particularly their constituent populations, into equilibrium with their environments. This is not to say that better, more adapted, individuals could not occur, but their evolution is limited by the amount of variation available. There may either not be the genetic variation available to allow natural selection to create populations of superior individuals, or the variation present may not be suitable for creating individuals which are superior in the existing habitat of the species.

Pollution, on the other hand, creates new environments. Suddenly the populations of a species are no longer in equilibrium with an environment they have long experienced. Conditions are completely new and we can see natural selection starting afresh to mould the species in a remarkable manner. To understand how this can occur, we must first look at the mechanism of evolution and one or two examples of selection in ordinary situations.

1.3 Types of variation

All characters are ultimately determined by genes; this ensures that there is continuity of characteristics between one generation and the next. Actual patterns of inheritance can differ however, depending on whether a character is determined by one or by several pairs of genes. When only one pair of genes is involved the pattern of inheritance is very simple although it was a considerable intellectual feat by Mendel to be

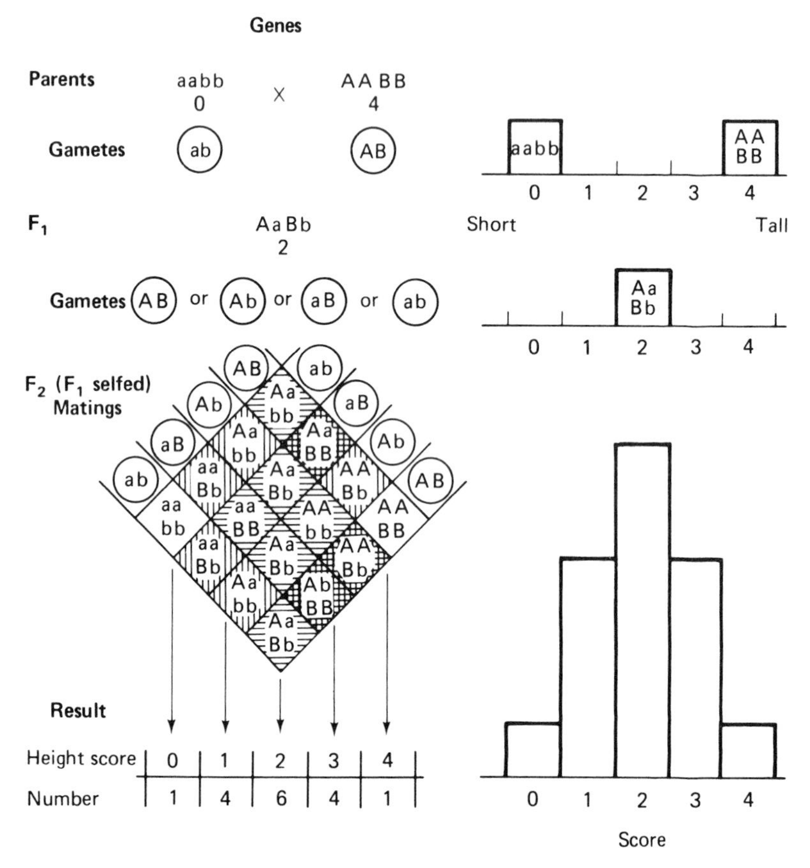

Fig. 1–2 The result of crossing pure breeding short and tall plants when the character is determined by two pairs of genes acting in an additive manner: there is a continuous range of variation in the F_2 generation. (Each capital letter represents an additive gene scoring one height unit.)

the first person to understand it. He worked with genes which had major effects on the garden pea. He showed that, for example, when a tall and a short plant were crossed, the progeny were all tall; shortness had effectively disappeared because tall was dominant. However when these tall plants were crossed, their progeny contained both tall and short plants, in a ratio of approximately 3 tall: 1 short. Although dominance can cause the character to disappear for a generation, it has the potential to reappear in any subsequent generation. When a character is determined by *major genes* like this the variation is *discontinuous* and easy to see.

Most characters in living organisms are, however, more complex since they are determined by several processes and therefore by several pairs of genes. In this case the resulting patterns of inheritance are more complex (and explain why biologists originally dismissed Mendel's proposals). But they can be understood if we assume the simplest situation in which the character is determined by only two pairs of genes, which are inherited independently of each other and whose effects add up to give the final character (Fig. 1–2). Now we have a situation which looks like blending inheritance, where the differences between the original parents seem to disappear as we progress from one generation to another. But this is not true because the continuous range of variability which appears in the second (F_2) generation is genetically determined, and if we breed from particular F_2 individuals we can get very different families in the next (F_3) generation. So when a character is determined by many genes with small effect, *polygenes*, although the variation is now *continuous*, it is still genetically determined, just as if it was discontinuous. This is because the individual polygenes are still behaving in a Mendelian manner.

1.4 Effects of selection

If a character is genetically determined it is heritable and can be selected for. The action of selection on a population containing a pair of major genes can easily be demonstrated if we know the fitness of the different genotypes – the relative amounts they contribute to the next generation. Figure 1–3 shows the change in the proportion of a gene present in a population (gene frequency) where individuals possessing that gene produce 20 % fewer offspring (i.e. their fitness is 20 % less) than individuals lacking the gene. What is surprising perhaps is that even with a difference in fitness as little as this the population changes markedly in few generations. If one genotype had been 40 % less fit than the other the rate of change would have been twice as fast.

When a character is determined by polygenes similar changes in gene frequency can occur. However we are unable to see individual gene effects and so must use the average characteristics of the population. In

1900 a selection experiment on corn (*Zea mays*) was set up in the University of Illinois, in which there was selection for high, and also for low, oil content in the grain in an old unselected variety, 'Burr White'. This experiment is still continuing. The results of the first fifty years (Fig.

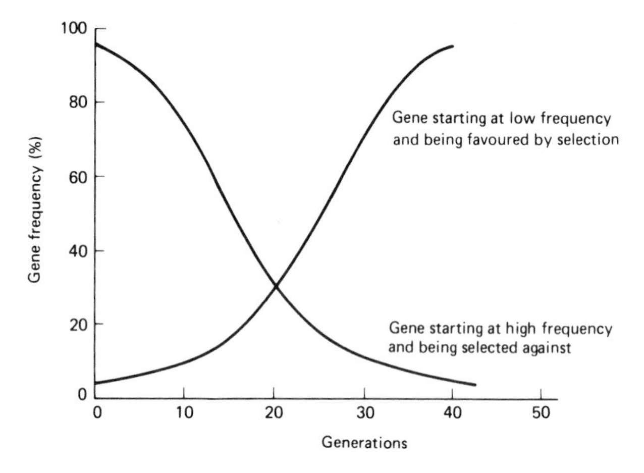

Fig. 1–3 The changes which occur in the frequency of a dominant gene which is either favoured or disfavoured by a selection intensity of 20%: the change in gene frequency is very rapid.

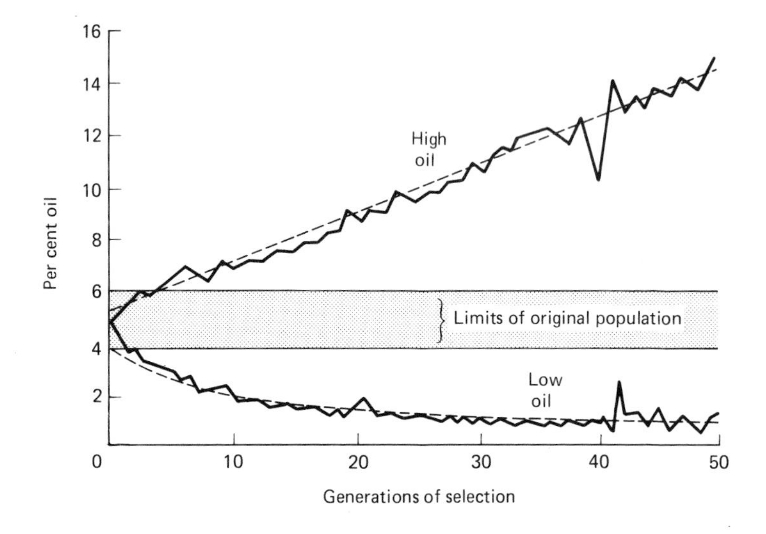

Fig. 1–4 The outcome of selection for high and low oil content in the Illinois corn experiment: response to selection is considerable (Woodworth, *et al.*, 1952; by permission of the American Society of Agronomy).

1–4) show that there is an enormous store of variability, which is available for selection, in a character determined by polygenes. In particular the two selected populations have reached levels of oil content which are far outside the range of the initial population.

This can be explained if some of the original variation was in the form AAbb and aaBB, each of which would score 2 in the scheme shown in Fig. 1–3. With crossing and subsequent recombination of genes, genotypes such as AABB and aabb would be produced
4 0
which would score more (or less) than their parents. This hidden, or transgressive segregation, as it is called, is now well understood (EDWARDS, 1977). Plant breeders, in particular, rely on it to achieve increases in yield. But it is also a widespread property of characters in natural populations, and, just as in maize under artificial selection, it allows populations to respond in remarkable ways to natural selection.

In the end, however, the store of genetic variation in a population available for selection must become exhausted, because the number of genes in the population is finite. Some new variability may arise due to gene mutation but this is a slow and largely unpredictable source. As a result a population being subjected to selection ultimately stops responding and reaches a plateau (Fig. 1–5). It will be unable to respond further unless it receives new genetic variation by mutation, or by hybridization with some related organism carrying different genes. It seems likely that most established populations are in the plateau situation, where they have run out of all immediately available variation of value in their existing environment.

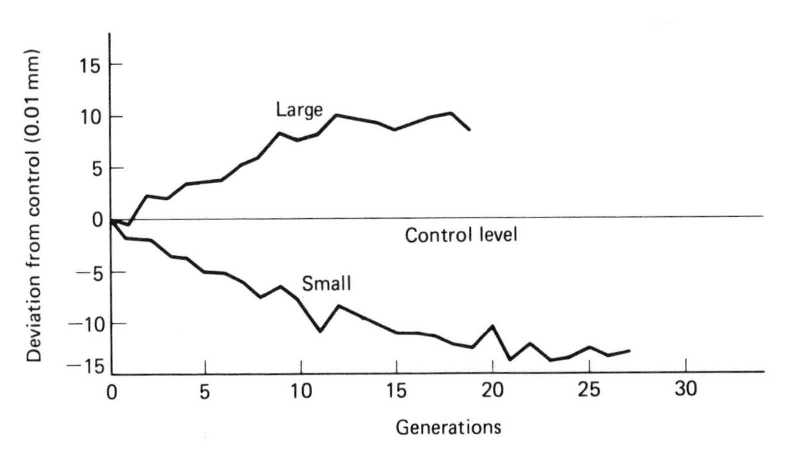

Fig. 1–5 The outcome of selection for body size (thorax length) in *Drosophila melanogaster*: eventually there is no further response to selection (ROBERTSON, 1955).

However we must not lose sight of the fact that what we see as a population in the field is a collection of phenotypes, the product of the effects of the environment on the expression of the genotype of an individual. These effects can make genetically different individuals look phenotypically similar and so prevent selection from acting on these *hidden genetic differences.*

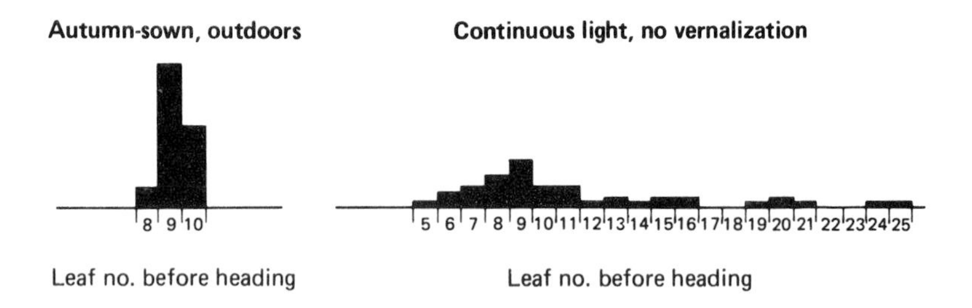

Fig. 1–6 Flowering time in a population of ryegrass grown in normal and abnormal conditions: an apparently uniform population reveals that it contains hidden variation when it is exposed to a new environment (COOPER, 1954).

If a population becomes subjected to a new environment, some of these genetic differences within it may now be revealed, for instance when a ryegrass population (*Lolium perenne*) is transferred to a new environment (Fig. 1–6). It can now respond again to selection. This will also happen when the population becomes exposed to a pollutant; in this changed environment new selective forces can now operate. Rapid responses to selection are possible, as we shall see in subsequent chapters.

2 Evolution in Natural Conditions

2.1 Effects on artificial populations

The power of selection in natural conditions can be demonstrated by very simple experiments. If an artificial mixture of different genotypes is sown out in a field under normal conditions, allowed to grow to maturity, the seed collected and re-sown the next year, the proportions of the different genotypes change very rapidly, and in a few generations some get completely eliminated. This was shown first by H. V. Harlan and M. J. Martini in a large scale experiment in the United States involving a mixture of barley varieties.

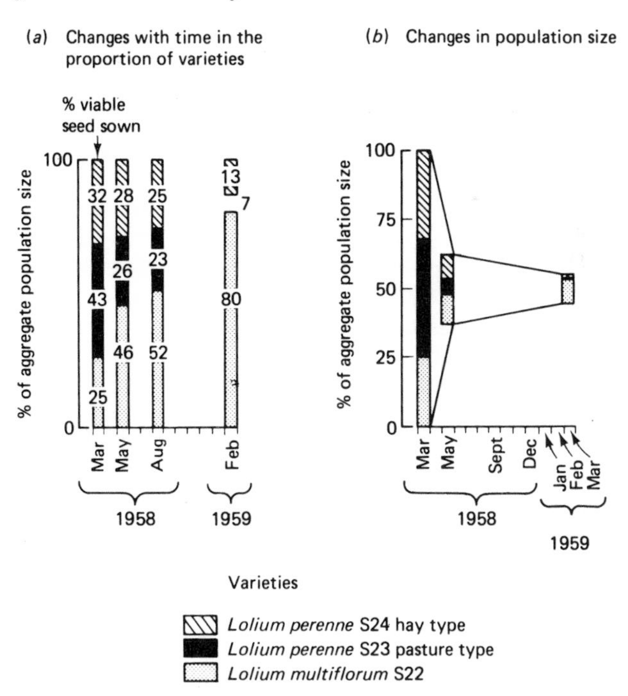

Fig. 2–1 Change in genotype frequency in a mixture of ryegrass varieties sown in natural conditions: population changes can occur within a single generation (CHARLES, 1961).

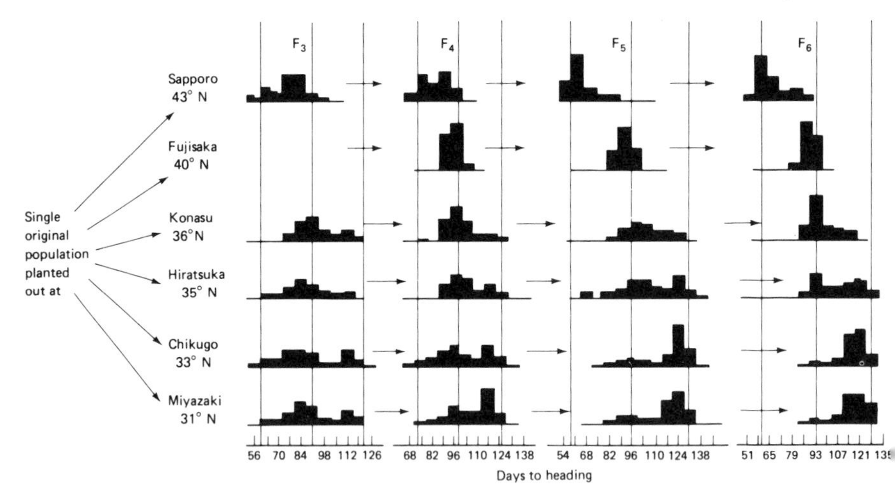

Fig. 2–2 Histograms of heading dates in a rice population grown for successive generations in different regions of Japan: the original population rapidly changes by natural selection to become completely different in each region (Akemine and Kikuchi in ALLARD and HANSCHE, 1964).

But recently CHARLES (1961) has shown that these sort of changes can occur within a single generation in a mixture of grass genotypes (Fig. 2–1). The rate of change is remarkable, particularly since it occurred in field conditions in a natural pasture. It could occur because initially more seedlings became established than could possibly survive later: change in genotype frequency was due to selective death of some individuals and their replacement in the sward by the continued growth of others. This, as Darwin observed many times, is a common occurrence: more seeds fall to the ground and germinate than can survive to become adults.

When a single population is sown under a variety of different conditions we can not only follow the genetic changes in individual populations but also the results of different natural selection in different places (Fig. 2–2). H. Akemine and F. Kikuchi made up a highly variable rice population by hybridizing two existing rice varieties. As a result the enormous power of natural selection for causing evolutionary change is made very clear. Not only do the populations in the different environments evolve in quite different directions, but they do so in very few generations.

2.2 Effects on species

When a wild species in the course of time enlarges its range it inevitably spreads into different, new, environments. Consequently, in each new situation it becomes subject to all the effects of each particular environment. Natural selection then begins to act, to refine each character of the species in relation to its new conditions of life. Darwin recognized this likelihood, very clearly, in the *Origin of Species* (Chapter IV).

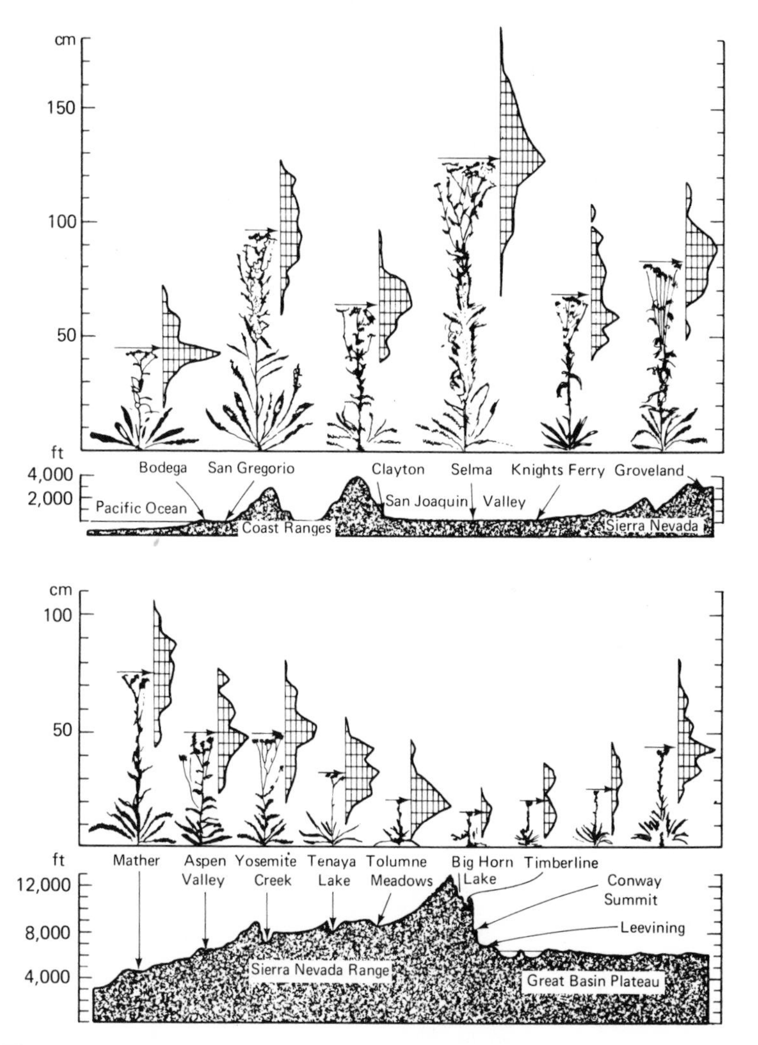

Fig. 2–3 Populations of yarrow from a west-to-east transect across central California grown in a single standard environment: the species is composed of very different populations, the result of natural selection (CLAUSEN, 1962; by permission of Cornell University Press).

As a result we find that species are differentiated into local, adapted, populations, called *ecotypes* by G. Turesson. One of the best examples is the work by J. Clausen, D. D. Keck and W. M. Hiesey on the common plant, yarrow (*Achillea lanulosa* and *A. borealis*) (Fig. 2–3). They showed that the populations are not only morphologically, but also physiologically, distinct. The alpine populations are more frost tolerant, flower more rapidly, are able to photosynthesize at lower temperatures, but are more sensitive to fungal disease, than lowland populations. This pattern has been shown to occur in many different species, such as bent grass (*Agrostis tenuis*), tormentil (*Potentilla glandulosa*), and cranesbill (*Geranium sanguineum*) (see BRIGGS and WALTERS, 1969).

Soil is a major part of the environment of plants. There is no reason therefore why soil differences should not cause the evolution of populations with considerable differences in adaption to soil factors. It is now known from the work of R. W. Snaydon, A. D. Bradshaw and others that such differentiation is widespread, in common (as well as rare) species such as white clover (*Trifolium repens*), cocksfoot (*Dactylis glomerata*), and sheep's fescue (*Festuca ovina*) (Fig. 2–4). So Darwin was more correct than he perhaps realized.

All these differences have been found in populations considerable distances apart (>1 km). Yet environments can change over distances of only a few metres. Can these cause the evolution of distinct populations? One might think that it was not possible, because the populations would be close enough to exchange genes by migration of pollen and seeds so

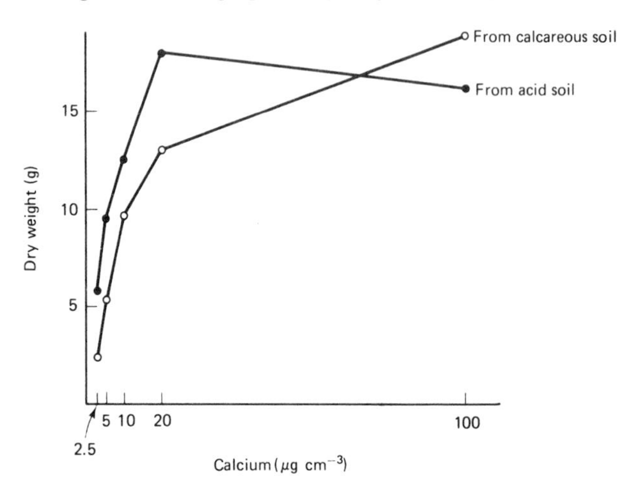

Fig. 2–4 The growth of two populations of sheep's fescue coming from contrasting soils, at various calcium levels: they have completely different patterns of response (SNAYDON and BRADSHAW, 1961).

that gene flow would counteract the effects of differential selection in adjacent environments. But a great deal of work on plants has shown that differentiation can occur in populations which are effectively

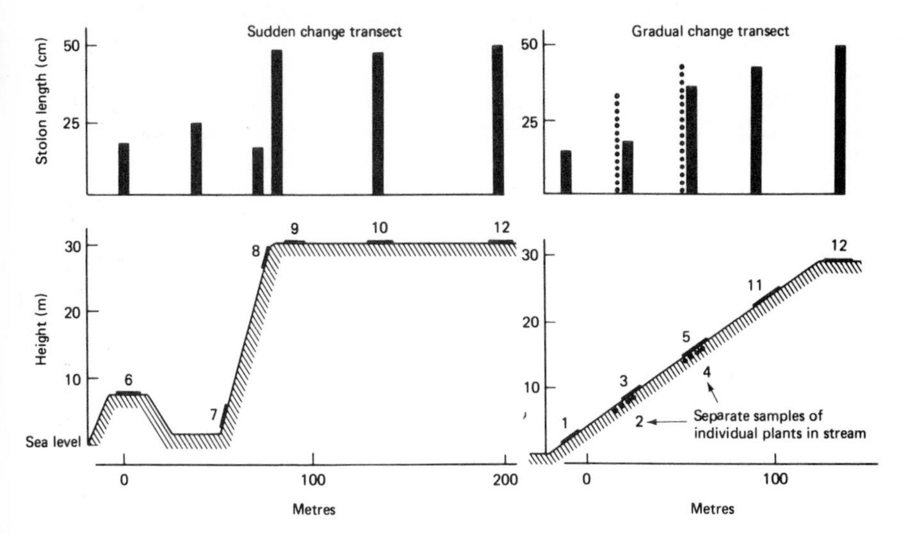

Fig. 2–5 The stolon lengths of populations of creeping bent grass (*Agrostis stolonifera*) taken from Abraham's Bosom Anglesey, N. Wales and grown in an experimental garden: the pattern of population differentiation follows the pattern of the environment closely (ASTON and BRADSHAW, 1966).

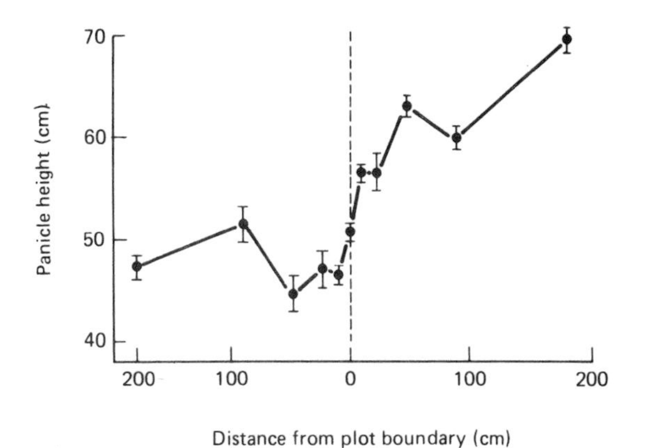

Fig. 2–6 The size in cultivation under standard conditions of plants of sweet vernal grass collected across the boundary between two plots of the Park Grass fertilizer experiment: the populations change over a distance of 10 cm (SNAYDON and DAVIES, 1976).

adjoining one another providing that the environments are sufficiently different (Fig. 2–5). The pattern of the environment determines completely the pattern of the evolutionary differentiation: where there are sharp boundaries population differences are sharp: where there are gradual changes in environment the population differences are also gradual, in the form of a cline.

There seems almost no limit to the sharpness of this differentiation providing that the environments are sharply separated. Davies and Snaydon have shown that in the liming experiment of the old Park Grass plots at Rothamsted, originally set up in 1903, the populations of sweet vernal grass (*Anthoxanthum odoratum*) change completely over a distance of only 10 cm (Fig. 2–6).

All these examples are important models for the possible effects of pollution, which in a very distinctive way can provide new habitats in which evolution can occur. We have become very familiar with the evolution of resistance in insects in relation to insecticides: control of some insect pests has now become extremely difficult (BROWN and PAL, 1971). Evolution of drug resistance in bacteria which are pathogenic to man is an ever present problem. Industrial melanism in insects is caused by the natural selection that occurs in the smoke laden environments of towns (FORD, 1976). Does anything similar occur in plants which are exposed to so many different sorts of pollution?

3 The Evolution Effects of Pollutants

3.1 Pollutants as selective agents

If pollutants are to cause evolutionary change it must be shown that

(*a*) pollutants have debilitating effects

(*b*) these effects occur differentially so that some individuals are more affected than others

(*c*) these differences are genetically determined.

The reason why we are concerned about pollutants is precisely because they *do* have debilitating effects on organisms (including ourselves). In extreme cases a pollutant can cause the death of whole plant communities. Nickel used to be refined at Sudbury, Ontario in the 1920s and 1930s by a process which involved burning the sulphide ore using iron sulphide as a fuel in long open roast heaps. The sulphur dioxide released killed the forest and all other vegetation downwind for a distance of 40 km: and without its protective plant cover the soil disappeared through erosion. Now, although the sulphur dioxide is led away in 150 m high stacks, the area remains derelict (Fig. 3–1).

The effects of pollutants, however, need not be so severe: plants can be only partly injured. There can still be visible injuries, because particular tissues are killed, but the plant as a whole survives. These injuries can be very characteristic for particular pollutants (Table 1). But sometimes the injury is invisible and all that occurs is a reduction in growth or yield. Ozone is produced as a result of photochemical oxidation processes occurring when nitrogen oxide compounds (NO_x), released into the atmosphere by motor vehicles, are exposed to bright sunlight. This causes characteristic brown lesions on the upper surfaces of leaves, but at the same time an overall reduction in yield, sufficient in Los Angeles, for instance, to make it completely uneconomic to grow citrus crops, although originally the crop was of major importance. Yield reductions can be observed in relation to most pollutants, such as when sulphur dioxide concentrations are more than about 0.1 p.p.m. SO_2 (300 μg m^{-3}) or PAN (peroxyacetyl nitrate) concentrations arising from motor vehicle exhausts are more than 0.01 p.p.m. (MELLANBY, 1980).

In these situations it is common to find that different species behave very differently. At the enormous nickel refinery at Falconbridge, Ontario, *Corylus cornuta* and *Vaccinium angustifolium* can still be found within 2 km, whereas *Pinus strobus* and *Trientalis americana* cannot any

Fig. 3–1 The wreckage caused by severe SO_2 pollution near the nickel refinery at Sudbury, Ontario: many years of emissions of SO_2 at ground level killed all the vegetation and allowed the soil to be washed away. (Photograph K. Winterhalder.)

Table 1 The effects of different pollutants.

Pollutant	*Occurrence*	*Symptoms*
SO_2 (sulphur dioxide)	Near to specific source or generally in urban areas in winter	Large collapsed areas around main veins visible on both surfaces usually ivory coloured: general chlorosis and premature senescence
O_3 (ozone)	Widespread in air influenced by cities in bright sunlight	Small necrotic spots on upper surface of leaves, interveinal streaks in monocots, grey or tan coloured
PAN (peroxyacetyl nitrate)	As ozone	Under surface of expanding leaves glazed or bronzed in a transverse band corresponding to time of highest incidence
HF (hydrogen fluoride)	Near to specific source	Necrosis of leaf tips and margins, grey green becoming reddish brown
Cu, Pb, Zn, etc. (heavy metals)	Near to specific ground or air source	Inhibition of root growth, widespread death of all but a few species, chlorosis if zinc or copper

longer be found less than 12 km away (GORHAM & GORDON, 1960). Differences *between species* must be of genetic origin: they therefore provide evidence that there is genetically determined variation in susceptibility to pollution. But variation at this level could be the incidental outcome of major differences in physiology and morphology which have no direct connection with pollution.

Variation in resistance or susceptibility to pollution found occurring *within species* is of much greater interest, since it could be the raw material on which natural selection could act. There is now a great deal of evidence for this. Individuals, as well as varieties and populations, of both wild and cultivated species have been discovered with resistance to pollution. Where resistance to pollution is found occurring naturally in whole *populations* the evolutionary arguments we have discussed in the last two chapters suggest that it is likely that this is due to the selective effects of pollution, as Prat suggested for copper mine red campion (*Silene dioica*). But the idea is easy to forget. The first record of natural populations differing in tolerance to air pollutants was published by DUNN in 1959. He found that populations of lupins (*Lupinus*) taken from urban areas of Los Angeles were much more resistant to the deleterious effects of smog than populations taken from unpolluted coastal areas, and suggested this was due to selection, a very reasonable suggestion. Yet this paper has been overlooked for twenty years.

Where resistance is found *between genotypes* within populations it is unlikely to have been put there by selection and must most truly represent the sort of genetic variation from which evolutionary changes could originate. The range of situations in which such variation has been reported is considerable, and we might wonder if there are any situations in which it does not occur.

Usually variation within populations appears as a continuous range of behaviour between the different individuals, no matter what the pollutant (Fig. 3–2). With this sort of variation, where the differences are not clear cut, it is difficult to be certain to what extent they are genetically determined. They could easily be due more to random environmental causes than to the joint action of many genes with small effect. This can best be checked by comparing the resistance of individual parent plants with the resistance of their offspring. If the differences between the parents are largely genetically determined they should be reflected in the offspring. The degree to which differences are genetically controlled (heritability) can be determined by the regression of the means of offspring on the means of their parents. When this was done for one population of *Geranium carolinianum* the heritability of resistance to SO_2 was found to be 50 % (Fig. 3–3). A similar situation is found in the tolerance to toxic metals discussed in Chapter 5.

Occasionally resistance to a pollutant is determined by a single pair of major genes. In this case the pattern of variation is clear cut, for instance

Table 2 Types of genetical variation in response to pollutants (BRADSHAW, 1976).

	Between genotypes	*Between populations*	*Between species*
Usual occurrence	At random within any populations of cultivated or wild plants, including between homozygous or vegetative varieties	In those populations subject to selection in polluted areas	At random, unless in relation to a natural pollution factor
Usual cause	Variation due to mutation and segregation	Systematic differences in gene frequently due to selection	Fortuitous characteristic, or side-effect of adaptation to other factors, unless in relation to a natural pollution factor
Notable examples	Susceptibility of Bel W_3 tobacco to ozone; resistance of different ryegrass genotypes to herbicides; different sensitivities of *Gladiolus* varieties to fluoride	Heavy metal tolerance in populations of many species; tolerance of Helmshore ryegrass to sulphur dioxide; tolerance of Glasgow populations of *Marchantia* to lead	Different sensitivities of lichens to sulphur dioxide; sensitivities of a wide range of species to sulphur dioxide; adaptation of *Ulva lactuca* to exploit high ammonium

in ozone resistance in onions (*Allium*). However this is unusual, and normally, as in white pine (*Pinus strobus*), tobacco (*Nicotiana tabacum*), and ryegrass (*Lolium perenne*) resistance to pollutants is a continuous varying character determined by many genes.

With genetically determined variability occurring, the evolution of resistance in populations exposed to pollution is obviously possible.

3.2 The evolutionary effects of SO_2

The most likely place to look for the evolution of resistance is in a population which is exposed to such high levels of pollution that the plants are obviously being damaged. In Coweta County, Georgia, U.S.A., there is a large old electricity generating station, Plant Yates, which burns high sulphur coal and emits its smoke from very low, 20 m, chimneys (Fig. 3–4).

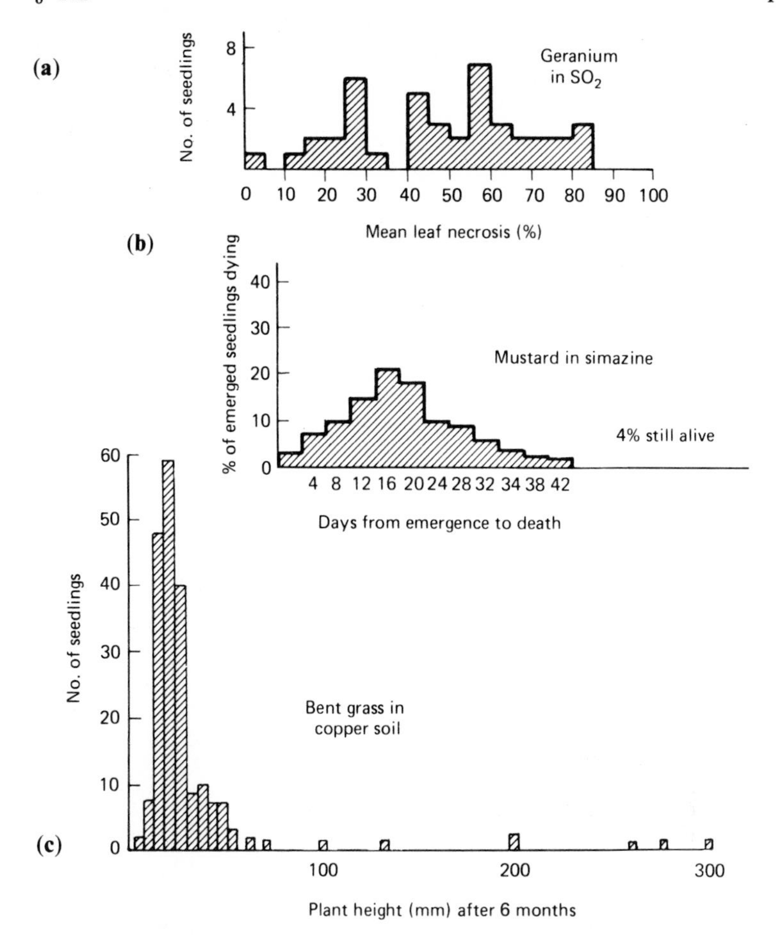

Fig. 3–2 Variability in normal populations in response to pollutants (**a**) in *Geranium carolinianum* exposed to SO_2 (**b**) in mustard (*Sinapis alba*) exposed to simazine (**c**) in bent grass (*Agrostis tenuis*) exposed to copper in the soil (TAYLOR and MURDY, 1975; KARIM and BRADSHAW, 1968; WALLEY *et al.*, 1974, respectively): in all cases there are considerable differences in the responses of individual plants.

The visible part of smoke is mainly particles of unburnt carbon. These are dirty and unpleasant but do not have major effects on plants. The important part of the smoke is the major invisible component, sulphur dioxide, formed from the oxidation of the sulphur contained in the coal. Coal usually contains 1–4 % sulphur: a 2000 megawatt power station can emit 600 tonnes of SO_2 per day. If this is emitted from chimneys less than 75 m high, it can readily cause ground level concentrations of

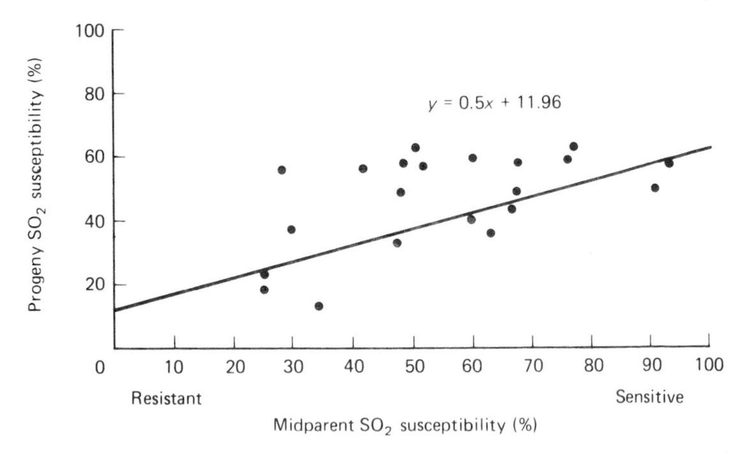

Fig. 3–3 Relationship, in susceptibility to SO_2, between parents and their offspring in *Geranium carolinianum*: it suggests a heritability of 50% (TAYLOR, 1978).

Fig. 3–4 Plant Yates, a coal fired electricity power station in Georgia U.S.A.: although there has been no serious damage the emissions of SO_2 from the low stacks have caused the evolution of resistant populations of *Geranium* and other species. (Photograph G. E. Taylor.)

1500 $\mu g\ SO_2\ m^{-3}$ (0.5 p.p.m.). If this level is maintained for more than a few hours all plants suffer and die. Average levels of 500 $\mu g\ m^{-3}$ reduce the growth of all plants, and sensitive species such as lichens and conifers are killed.

At Plant Yates there is severe damage to the trees surrounding the power station, and even low growing weeds such as *Geranium*

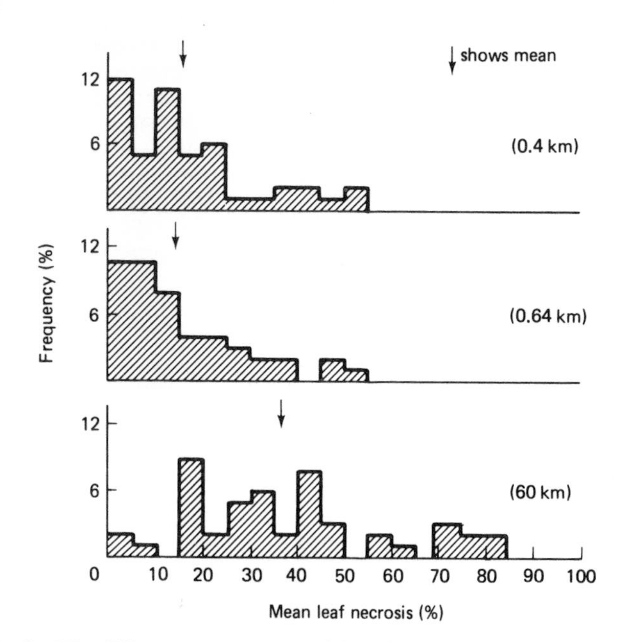

Fig. 3–5 The different responses to SO_2 of populations of *Geranium caroliniianum* from sites at different distances from a polluting power station: the near populations show considerable resistance. (TAYLOR and MURDY, 1975.)

carolinianum, *Plantago aristata*, hop trefoil *Trifolium campestre* and *Oxalis dilenii* show leaf lesions and necrosis. Collections of seeds of populations of *G. carolinianum* growing at different distances from the station were made by Taylor and Murdy. Plants were raised and exposed to 1560 $\mu g\ m^{-3}$ for 8–12 h in controlled chambers. Very clear differences in behaviour of the populations are apparent (Fig. 3–5). Individuals in populations collected less than 1 km from the station remained almost unaffected by the treatment: individuals from the other populations are variously affected. We have already seen that SO_2 tolerance in *Geranium* can be heritable (Fig. 3–3). It appears that natural selection in populations 1 and 2 has eliminated all the susceptible individuals leaving a population composed of tolerant genotypes.

But SO_2 pollution can also be more diffuse. Severe air pollution in Britain started with the industrial revolution. The main energy source, coal, meant that smoke was emitted from innumerable small inefficient furnaces forming a continuous pall over the industrial northern cities and countryside. Mean levels of SO_2 in winter of 500 $\mu g\ m^{-3}$ were commonplace, not enough to kill vegetation completely, but sufficient to cause the disappearance of all lichen species. Since World War II levels have been falling so that winter means are now

Table 3 Growth of a normal cultivar (S23) and selected clones from Helmshore of ryegrass in different SO_2 levels for 26 weeks (BELL and MUDD, 1976).

Material	*Control* (9 $\mu g\ SO_2\ m^{-3}$)	*Polluted* (191 $\mu g\ SO_2\ m^{-3}$)
Normal (S23)	1.296 (100)	0.653 (50)
Helmshore (selected)	1.388 (100)	1.377 (99)

Dry weight of shoots (g) and % of control.

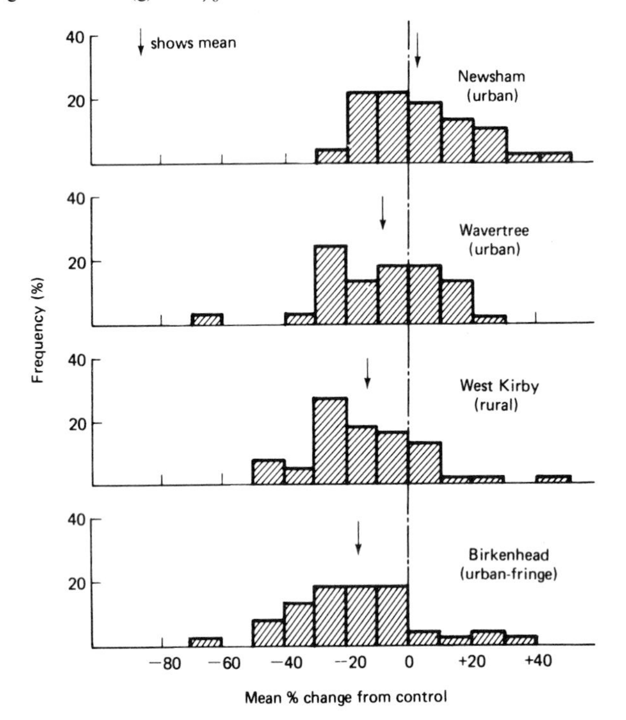

Fig. 3–6 The response of four ryegrass populations from Merseyside to SO_2 measured by growth in 650 $\mu g\ SO_2\ m^{-3}$ as % of growth in control (35 $\mu g\ m^{-3}$): there has been evolution of SO_2 tolerance in the city populations. (HORSMAN, ROBERTS and BRADSHAW, 1979.)

about 150 $\mu g\ m^{-3}$. Nevertheless in the 1960s, in a government agricultural experimental farm at Helmshore in the Pennines north of Manchester, Mudd noticed that the ryegrass (*Lolium perenne*) in the pastures sown from commercial seed always looked much worse after the winter than the ryegrass in the old natural pastures. Of course this could be because the local ryegrass was better adapted to the poor climatic conditions – Helmshore is at 400 m. However a selection from the native material was shown to be distinctly more tolerant to SO_2 than normal cultivars, which turn out to be sensitive to low levels of SO_2 (Table **3**).

Ryegrass is a common grass and is found in most areas where SO_2 levels have been high in the past. The results of Bell and Mudd suggest that perhaps the reason why it has survived in high SO_2 areas is because whole populations have evolved tolerance to SO_2. Tests on the populations growing at Helmshore and in the Merseyside area (Fig. 3–6) have recently shown that this is true. There is clear evolution of tolerance, which is localized to the most polluted areas.

The picture is therefore similar to that in *Geranium carolinianum* but we are not dealing with populations of a species persisting into high SO_2 levels produced by a local source, but of a common species in a general grassland occurring in normal urban pollution. It seems likely that evolution of this kind is widespread, wherever high SO_2 levels have occurred. The ryegrass cultivar, 'Manhattan', which originates from Central Park, New York, is as tolerant as the Newsham Park, Merseyside, population. We have no idea yet of the situation in other species but tolerance must surely occur. This tolerance could be important for agriculture in polluted areas: we shall consider this in Chapter 8.

3.3 The evolutionary effects of herbicides

Modern agriculture has relied heavily for the past thirty years upon the use of herbicides to control the multitude of weeds which invade our crops. As a result, although not strictly pollutants, herbicides must constitute strong selective agents equivalent in their effects to heavy metals and sulphur dioxide. If we repeat our basic theme, that if the appropriate genetic variation is present in a species, strong selection pressures can bring about changes in population structure, we can ask whether such variation in herbicide susceptibility occurs in weed populations, and whether herbicide resistant weeds have evolved.

Many species of weeds have, in fact, been shown to exhibit considerable variation in susceptibility to herbicides and will respond to artificial selection. So the basic material for the evolution of resistant weeds exists. Now the actual evolution has been reported. A very high degree of resistance to the triazine group of herbicides has been found in weed populations in North America.

The first report was of a population of groundsel (*Senecio vulgaris*) taken from a nursery in Washington which had been treated continuously with atrazine or simazine, both triazine herbicides. It was found to grow normally in atrazine levels of 2–4 kg ha^{-1}, which are completely lethal to normal populations of the same species (RYAN, 1970). Similarly

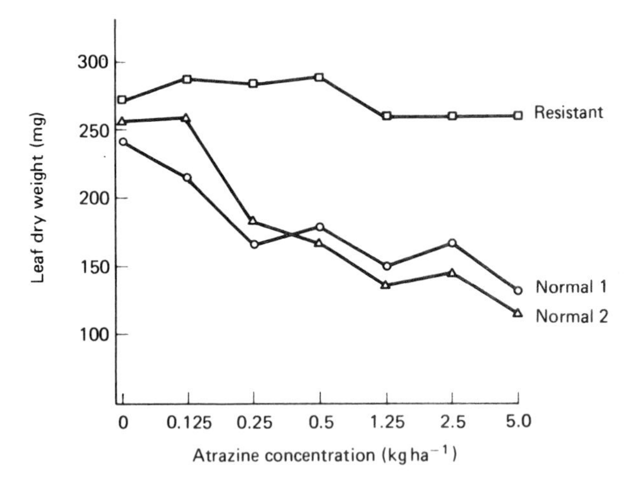

Fig. 3–7 The effect of different levels of the herbicide atrazine on resistant and normal populations of fat hen: leaves remain normal in the resistant population (MARRIAGE and WARWICK, 1980).

fat hen (*Chenopodium album*) populations resistant to triazine herbicides have been found in cornfields in Canada (BANDEEN and MCLAREN, 1976). Resistant and susceptible plants take up similar amounts of herbicide, but in resistant plants the chloroplasts and leaf growth are unaffected (Fig. 3–7). Originally, resistant populations were rare and unimportant: but now there are, for example, 200 000 ha of resistant groundsel in Washington, and 90 000 ha of resistant fat hen in Ontario with new occurrences being reported every year.

In the United Kingdom so far, despite a lot of searching, resistance is very rare. Only one resistant population of groundsel has been found, in an area of soft fruit, which shows the same degree of resistance as the American groundsel. Nonetheless considerable variation in response to simazine has been found in many populations of groundsel, and fat hen (Table 4) as well as in shepherd's purse (*Capsella bursa-pastoris*). The degree of resistance is closely related to the length of time the herbicide has been used, i.e. the number of generations of selection. So if appropriate variation exists for evolution of full tolerance to simazine in groundsel populations in the United Kingdom, why has not full tolerance evolved widely as it has in North America?

It seems that the reason relates firstly to the ways in which the herbicides are used. In the U.S., simazine is used as a pre-emergence herbicide – to kill seedlings as they germinate – and is followed by use of the closely related herbicide atrazine to kill off any surviving seedlings. Thus a consistent selection pressure has been applied over a

Table 4 Variation in susceptibility to the herbicide simazine in soil, of populations of groundsel and fat hen (HOLLIDAY and PUTWAIN, 1977).

Population	*No. of years treatment*	*% survival*
Groundsel		
1 Sudbury, Suffolk	10	13.1
2 Sudbury, Suffolk	8	6.7
3 Sittingborne, Kent	6	1.6
4 Malpas, Cheshire	6	99.8
Fat hen		
1 Invergourie, Fife	1	12.2
2 Maidstone, Kent	4	77.9
3 Peckham, Kent	9	77.4

ten year period and completely resistant populations have evolved. In the United Kingdom on the other hand, weed populations being treated with a triazine herbicide are almost invariably given a second quite different herbicide later, e.g. pre-emergence simazine followed by post-emergence paraquat. So the selection imposed upon the weed populations is not consistent through time, and the potential for evolution of full simazine resistance is greatly reduced. Dual resistance is extremely rare and individuals surviving treatment by the first herbicide are killed by the second.

The second reason relates to the genetic basis of herbicide resistance. American groundsel populations are resistant due to the action of a single major gene, which causes a biochemical detoxification of the simazine. United Kingdom populations however have resistance controlled by a series of polygenes' and changes in a number of biochemical pathways may be involved. In which case evolution of full resistance will be slower and less certain. Nevertheless resistant populations are appearing. At one time when herbicides had only just been invented we had the idea that weeds were a thing of the past. There was even a symposium on crop production in a weed-free environment. The future is not so certain.

4 Metal Pollution and Evolution

4.1 Soils and the heavy metals

Garden or agricultural soils normally contain at least trace quantities of the heavy metals copper, lead, nickel and zinc adsorbed onto clays, organic matter, and hydrous oxides of iron, aluminium and manganese. The total levels of these metals do not usually exceed 200–300 $\mu g\ g^{-1}$ and they never, therefore, reach such a concentration as would render them toxic.

There are however certain areas of the world, such as in Rhodesia and Australia where the presence of undisturbed ore bodies near the soil surface create soils which naturally contain toxic levels of the heavy metals. These are termed 'anomalies' by geochemists. In Europe and the British Isles naturally occurring ore bodies have long been exploited through mining by man, certainly since early Roman times. There is recent evidence that Neolithic man exploited copper rich ores as long ago as 4500 B.C. in Austria, Bulgaria, Spain, and probably Ireland. These activities were on a relatively localized and small scale. However, the mining industry in Britain developed, and reached a peak during the late eighteenth and first half of the nineteenth centuries. Separation of the wanted ore from other materials in the parent rock always presented a problem, and often the associated less valuable metals, such as the zinc which occurs commonly with lead, were discarded onto waste tips together with the other inert materials. This means that the tips of mine waste can contain considerable quantities of toxic metals. Table 5 gives the results of the analysis of some mine spoils and, for comparison, data showing the ranges expected in normal soils. It is very clear that not only do the spoils contain large quantities of heavy metals, but that they are also very low in nitrogen and phosphorus, although they contain adequate quantities of potassium. In addition they are in many cases made up mainly of particles with the dimensions of sand and gravel, and contain negligible quantities of organic matter.

The low level of nitrogen in mine spoils may be related to their large particle size allowing free drainage, and the high solubility of nitrates in percolating waters. Heavy metal phosphates are practically insoluble, and hence their availability in mine spoils will be extremely low. In normal soils organic matter acts as a reservoir for nutrients, both within the material and by adsorption; it also improves water retention. Since it is very low or absent in mine spoils both nutrient and water retention capacities are very poor. Organic matter can also form stable complexes

Table 5 Chemical analyses of some mine spoils from the British Isles, and the ranges found in normal soils. Values are total content of air dried material, as $\mu g\ g^{-1}$.

Site	*pH*	*Pb*	*Zn*	*Cu*	*N*	*P*	*K*
Minera, Clwyd	7.3	14 000	34 000	625	164	97	1960
Y Fan, Powys	4.5	42 400	6700	376	122	245	3400
Parys Mountain, Gwynedd	3.6	327	124	2060	88	141	2670
Goginan, Dyfed	5.4	16 800	2700	134	120	103	458
Ecton, Staffordshire	7.2	29 900	20 200	15 400	110	116	825
Snailbeach, Salop	7.2	20 900	20 500	25	100	110	1780
Darley, Derbyshire	7.3	6000	4600	80	32	93	1550
Normal soils	4.5–6.5	2–200	10–300	100–200	200–2000	200–3000	500–3500

with heavy metal ions; in sufficient quantity it can render toxic soils non-toxic, by making the heavy metals unavailable to plants.

It is clear then that mine spoils present most inhospitable environments for plant growth. To the student of evolution on the other hand they present a marvellous situation in which plant and animal populations have in many cases in the recent past been exposed to a new set of harsh environmental factors, and hence strong forces of selection.

4.2 Plant populations on toxic soils

In spite of the extreme inhospitality of mine spoils, it is rare to find them devoid of vegetation (Fig. 4–1). They are however generally characterised by the sparseness of their vegetation with a great deal of bare ground between established plants. In many cases mine spoils occur adjacent to non toxic soils supporting normal vegetation. This means that seed from this vegetation, as well as that produced by the plants growing on the mine spoil, will be potential colonizers of the mine spoil. In spite of this, and the fact that many mines have been in existence for 200 years or more, they remain largely uncovered by plants; by contrast the Broadbalk field at Rothamsted, left uncultivated since 1856 now supports mixed oak woodland. Why are mine spoils not similarly covered in vegetation? How do some plants colonize these sites apparently quite readily?

4.3 Metal tolerance in plant populations

In attempting to begin to answer such questions, we must return to the work of Prat which was mentioned in Chapter 1. This led him to believe

Fig. 4–1 Plants growing on toxic lead/zinc mine waste at Minera Mine, Clwyd: despite the toxicity some species survive, because they have evolved tolerance.

that the red campion (*Silene dioica*) plants growing on the mine in Austria were the product of natural selection in response to the toxic mine habitat. This very elegant piece of work remained largely ignored until 1952 when Bradshaw showed that if adult bent grass plants collected from a lead mine were grown in soil from the mine they grew well and flourished. If material of the same species taken from a pasture was planted in the mine soil, the plants became chlorotic and eventually died. He further found that the roots of the mine plants in the mine soil were strong and healthy, whereas the pasture plant roots stopped growing when the transplant was made. The heavy metals had an immediate and marked effect on root growth of normal plants.

A culture technique to show this effect was developed by D. A. Wilkins in 1957 for grass species. This involved comparison of root growth in solutions with, and without, added metal salts. The effects of various concentrations of copper and of zinc on root growth of mine and pasture populations of common bent grass (*Agrostis tenuis*) and bladder campion (*Silene vulgaris*) are shown in Fig. 4–2. The technique or modification of it has been widely used to examine populations of many plant species from mine and pasture habitats.

Usually, for grass species, separate single shoots (tillers) of an individual plant are grown in two solutions, one the control, containing hydrated calcium nitrate at $0.5\ \mathrm{g\,l^{-1}}$ to encourage root growth, the other

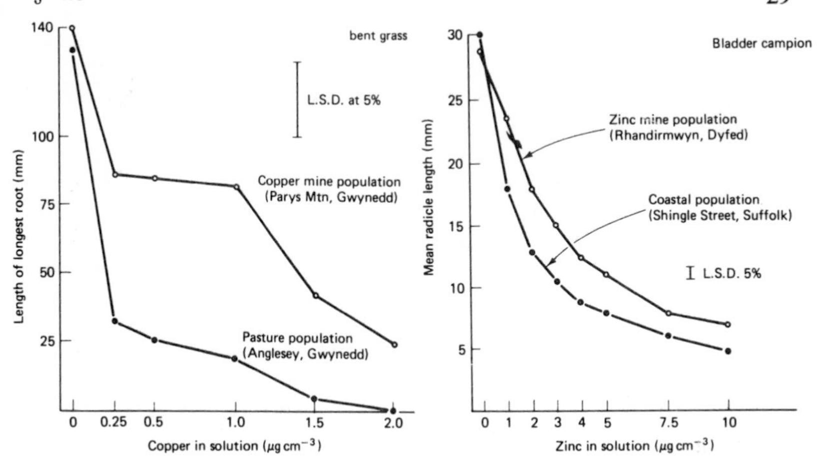

Fig. 4–2 The effect of copper and zinc on root growth of copper mine and zinc mine and non-mine plants of (**a**) bent grass and (**b**) bladder campion: rooting is more affected in the normal populations (MCNEILLY and BRADSHAW, 1968; BAKER, 1978).

Table 6 Levels of metals commonly used in tolerance tests.

Metal	*Metal level in test solution* ($\mu g\,cm^{-3}$)	*Salt*	*Salt concentration in stock solution* ($g\,l^{-1}$)
Copper	0.5	$CuSO_4.5H_2O$	0.393
Zinc	7.5	$ZnSO_4.7H_2O$	0.660
Lead	12.0	$Pb(NO_3)_2$	3.837
Nickel	2.0	$NiSO_4.7H_2O$	1.913

In each case 5 ml of stock solution should be made up to 1 litre with a hydrated calcium nitrate solution containing 0.5 $g\,l^{-1}$. This will give the appropriate level of the metal in the test solution.

being the control solution to which is added the salt of the appropriate heavy metal. A list of the more commonly used levels for copper, lead, nickel and zinc are given in Table 6. Regular changes of solution ensure aeration and maintenance of solution metal levels. After two weeks growth the lengths of the longest roots produced in each solution are measured, and from this an index of tolerance is calculated:

$$\frac{\text{Mean longest root length in control solution + metal}}{\text{Mean longest root length in control solution}} \times 100$$

Clearly the greater the root length made in the solution containing the metal the greater the index of tolerance. It has been shown that in general the greater the level of the particular heavy metal in the mine spoil from which the plant was taken the greater the index of tolerance. Plants from normal soils produce the shortest roots in the metal containing solution, and have a low index of tolerance.

Using this test it is possible to produce a quantitative character, the index of tolerance, in the same way as plant height, leaf width, or protein content are measured. The metal tolerance of populations of plants from any habitat can also be represented by histograms. Figure 4–3 shows histograms of tolerance indices for non-tolerant pasture and tolerant copper mine populations.

Using this rooting technique or modifications of it, plant populations have been found which are tolerant to cadmium, copper, lead, nickel, zinc, aluminium, and manganese when these elements are present at toxic levels in the soils in which the plants have been growing. Some plant populations have even evolved tolerance to arsenic on the sites of old arsenic smelters. Tolerance has been shown to be a characteristic of populations within a species, and not of whole species.

It is also clear that metal tolerance is a continuously varying character (like plant height in Chapter 1) and is probably controlled by more than one gene.

The almost universal occurrence of metal tolerant populations on mine spoils shows the remarkable power of natural selection as a force for evolutionary change in response to changed environmental factors.

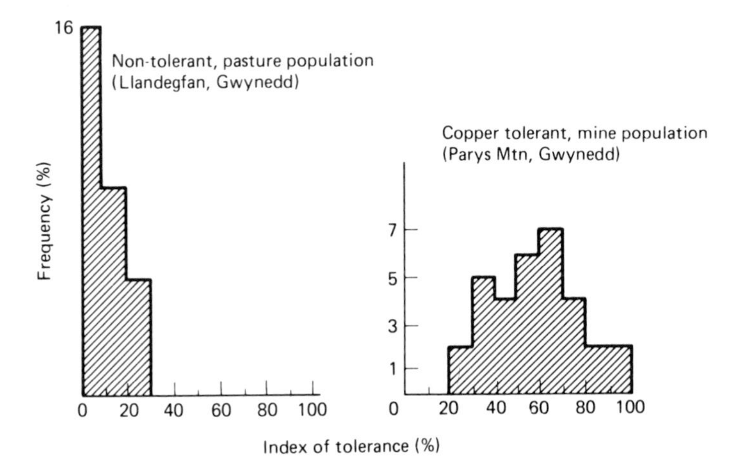

Fig. 4–3 Index of tolerance values for a normal and a copper-tolerant population of bent grass. The mean index of tolerance of the normal population is only 10 % of the mine population 60 %.

4.4 Tolerance to more than one metal

Tolerance is specific to any one metal. Thus copper tolerant plants do not show enhanced tolerance to lead or to zinc, and *vice versa*. There is however one exception to this general rule, and that is that populations which show zinc tolerance almost invariably show some tolerance to nickel, regardless of whether nickel was present in the spoil from which the plants came.

It is not uncommon, however, to find mine spoils which contain toxic amounts of more than one heavy metal. Lead and zinc almost always occur together in ore bodies. Parts of the very large copper mine at Parys Mountain, Anglesey, were exploited for lead, although for most of its life it was the largest copper mine in the world.

The spoil produced at such mines therefore frequently contain toxic levels of lead and zinc, or copper and lead. Plants are able to colonize such spoils, and, just as natural selection has been able to produce populations of plants tolerant to a single metal, so the plants from spoil containing, lead and zinc, or copper and lead, are tolerant to both metals

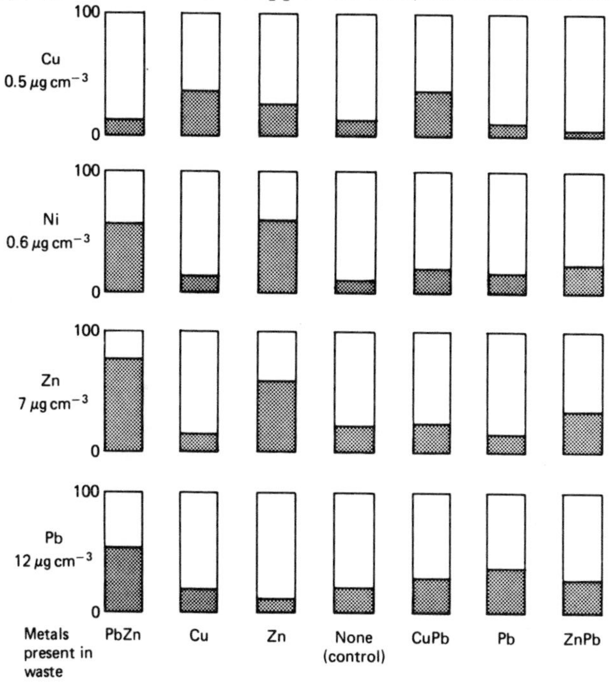

Fig. 4–4 The mean indices of tolerance of a number of metals of populations of bent grass from areas contaminated by different metals (GREGORY and BRADSHAW, 1965).

(Fig. 4–4). More recently SIMON (1977) in Belgium has shown that zinc- and lead-tolerant ecotypes of sheeps fescue (*Festuca ovina*) are also tolerant to cadmium present in the mine spoil.

4.5 The mechanism of tolerance

A great deal of work has been carried out examining various aspects of heavy metals and their effects on plants. The physiology of tolerant plants has only begun to receive attention relatively recently, however. What does this tell us of the mechanism of tolerance?

The possession of a mechanism which excludes the metals from the plant would be a most effective system. Although this has been shown in the green alga *Chlorella*, in higher plants heavy metals are taken up and occur throughout the plant. The roots of tolerant plants contain no less metal, and usually more, than non-tolerant plants. No exclusion mechanism therefore operates. But the shoots of both tolerant and non-tolerant plants generally contain less metal than the roots, and with the passage of time the levels appearing in the shoots of non-tolerant plants are more than in tolerant plants. This is particularly clear in copper-tolerant plants (Fig. 4–5). This suggests that there could be some mechanism in the roots, particularly of tolerant plants, which restricts metal movement to the rest of the plant.

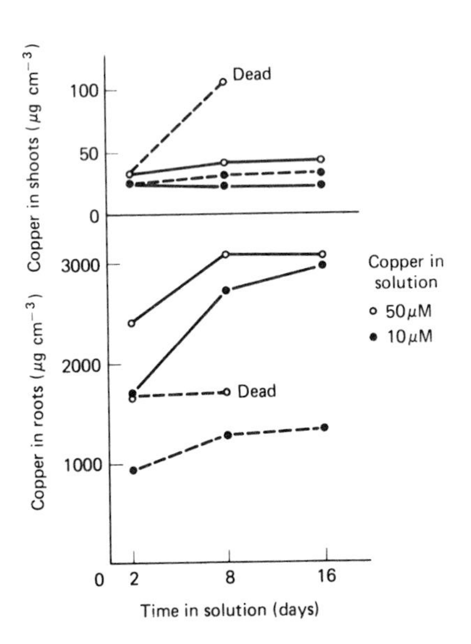

Fig. 4–5 The uptake of copper by tolerant (solid lines) and non-tolerant (dashed lines) clones of bent grass. (After WU, THURMAN and BRADSHAW, 1975).

What happens to the metals once in the plant? It has been shown that copper- and zinc-tolerant plants accumulate metals mainly in the cell walls, and that the amount of metal accumulated is directly related to the index of tolerance of the plants. The heavy metals appear to be bound as a stable complex with either a pectin-like or a proteinaceous substance. However when root segments of zinc-tolerant plants have been saturated with zinc and are unable to adsorb further zinc ions root growth has been found to continue, suggesting that the complexing of metals in roots cannot account for the whole of the metal tolerance mechanism.

More recent studies of sweet vernal grass (*Anthoxanthum odoratum*) and tufted hair grass (*Deschampsia caespitosa*) have shown that zinc-tolerant plants actively remove a large part of their absorbed zinc to the cell vacuole by transporting it across the tonoplast. In non-tolerant plants by contrast this does not occur because low levels of zinc inhibit zinc movement across the tonoplast. Once in the cytoplasm of non-tolerant plants zinc combines with enzymes and other important molecules and would thus rapidly inhibit cell processes. In tolerant

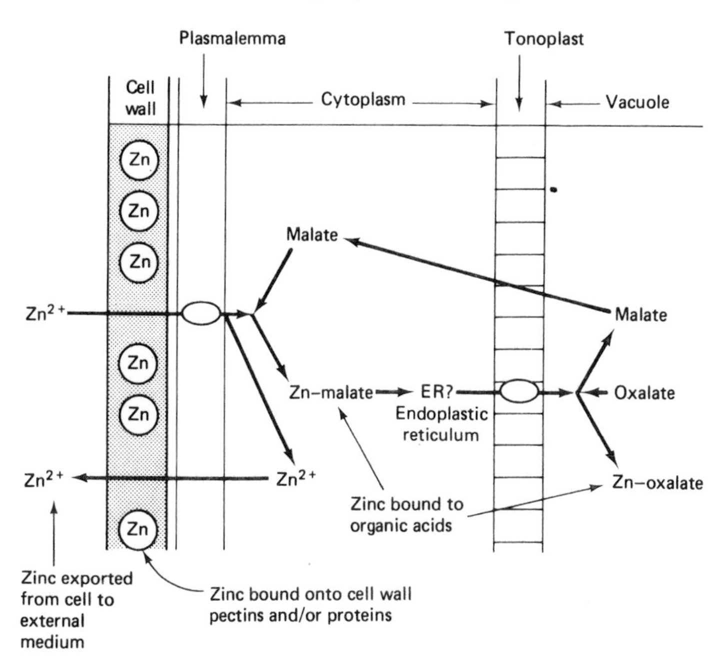

Fig. 4–6 Model incorporating currently proposed components of a zinc tolerance mechanism: there are three major mechanisms (based on MATHYS, 1977).

plants there appear to be sites at membranes which bind zinc, and render it harmless. The tolerant plants, unlike tolerant plants, are also able to maintain a continuing transport of internal zinc to the external medium, enabling the internal concentration of ionic and hence toxic zinc to be maintained at a lower level than in non-tolerant plants.

The internal complexing of the heavy metals may be due to the formation of heavy metal malates. Zinc-tolerant plants of bent grass (*Agrostis stolonifera*), sweet vernal grass (*Anthoxanthum odoratum*), tufted hair grass (*Deschampsia caepitosa*), bladder campion (*Silene vulgaris*) and sorrel (*Rumex acetosa*) have been shown to be able to produce considerably greater quantities of malate than non-tolerant plants in response to toxic levels of zinc. This factor has led Mathys (Fig. 4–6) to postulate a possible mechanism for zinc tolerance. However such a mechanism would not be zinc specific, one of the consistent features of heavy metal tolerance, as we have seen.

It would appear that no one mechanism of heavy metal tolerance exists and several different mechanisms, each promoting some degree of tolerance would seem likely to occur in combination to achieve full tolerance. It is interesting that if more than one mechanism is involved, then the genetic basis of tolerance is unlikely to be due to a single major gene.

5 The Genetic Basis of Metal Tolerance

5.1 Heritability

W. Johannsen very clearly showed that variation in an organism is due to genetic effects resulting from variation in genotype, and to environmental effects. These two together give rise to variations in the phenotype or appearance of the organism. We can represent this by a simple equation:

V_P	=	V_G	+	V_E
Phenotypic variation		Genetically caused variation		Environmentally caused variation

As we saw in Chapter 1, Darwin's explanation of evolution is that the effects of differential survival (natural selection) accumulate in populations. For this to happen features conferring adaptive advantage must be passed on from generation to generation; only inherited, genetically caused, characters are of importance in evolutionary change. Selection acts on the phenotype and it is only the variation in the phenotype which is genetically determined that is important for selection. It is clearly important, therefore, in studies of natural selection to know the extent to which variation in a character is due to genetic as opposed to environmental causes; in other words how accurately differences in phenotype reflect differences in genotype. The ratio genotypic/phenotypic variation is known as broad sense heritability, $h^2{}_B$, and using our simple equation above,

$$h^2{}_B = \frac{V_G}{V_P}$$

A knowledge of broad sense heritability is useful in interpreting data about variation in plant or animal populations since it indicates the proportion of the variation in a character which is genetically determined. As we saw in Chapter 1, however, genetic variation can be due to the action of major genes, or of polygenes with additive effects. Mendel's first law states that of a pair of alleles only one is passed into the gametes of an individual, and we know that they are passed on in a random way to offspring. But with dominance the characteristics of individual diploid genotypes are not passed on intact from generation to generation. In contrast, the additive value of a polygene is transmitted from a parent to its offspring in a regular and predictable way. It is clear then that the contribution of additive genetic variation to change brought about by selection will be considerably greater than that due to genetic variation involving dominance.

The proportion of the total phenotypic variability that is due to additive genetic effects is termed narrow sense heritability h^2_N. Its magnitude governs the extent of similarity between parents and offspring in a similar way to broad sense heritability, but because it refers to the additive component only – the variation due to individual genes – it enables us to predict the success of selection, whether natural or artificial. Clearly the higher the narrow sense heritability the greater the proportion of additive genetic variation and the greater response to selection. Figure 5–1 shows the importance of h^2_N in determining response to selection for two characters in hens, one, number of eggs laid, which has a low narrow sense heritability, ($h^2_N = 0.25$), the other, average egg weight, which has a high narrow sense heritability ($h^2_N = 0.75$).

It is clear then that studies of population differentiation in response to selection should include information on the genetic basis of the characters being investigated. What then do we know of the genetic basis of heavy metal tolerance in plants?

5.2 Simple methods of analysis

The simplest illustration that variation in a character or group of characters is genetically determined can be obtained merely by growing seed, collected from different plants in the wild, under standard environmental conditions and carrying out any investigations on these plants. Differences which persist in the offspring of different plants are assumed to be under genetic control.

To get a precise measure of heritability however it is usual to compare parents with their offspring (FALCONER, 1960). If the mean characteristics of groups of offspring with the same parents are plotted against the mean characteristics of their parents, the degree of relationship, measured by the coefficient of regression (which is merely the slope of the line through the points) gives a direct measure of the heritability (narrow sense) of the character.

All that therefore requires to be added to the previous approach is to collect samples of adult plants as well as samples of their progeny and grow them under standard environmental conditions, so that the characters of both generations can be assessed together. The value for the female parent can then be plotted against the mean value of the sample of its progeny. The coefficient of regression now provides an estimate of

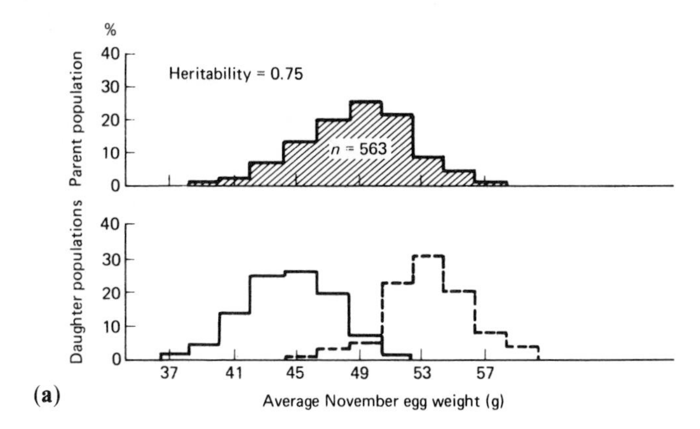

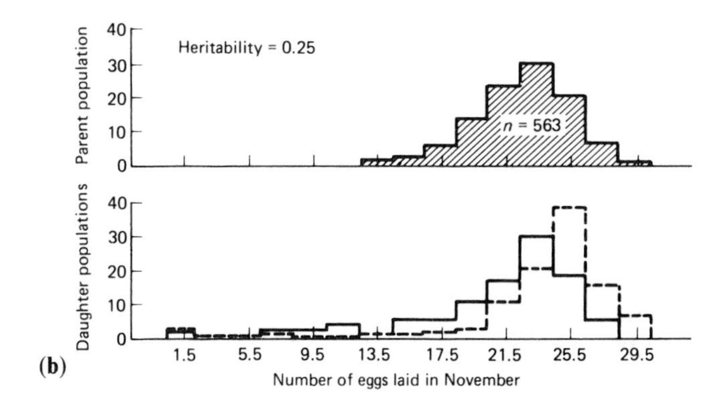

Fig. 5–1 The relationship between response to selection and heritability in the narrow sense, in two characteristics of egg production in hens. (**a**) Selection for increased and decreased egg weight, where heritability is high, causes considerable differences in the next generation. (**b**) Selection for increased and decreased egg number, where heritability is low, does not (LERNER, 1958).

half the narrow sense heritability. It is only half because the characters of only the female parent are known.

Such a technique is shown by the data in Fig. 5–2 for zinc tolerance in tufted hair grass (*Deschampsia caespitosa*). The estimated half narrow sense heritability is 0.59, showing us that most of the variation in zinc tolerance is due to additive gene effects. Clearly it is a character which should show a rapid response to selection, something we shall examine in Chapter 6.

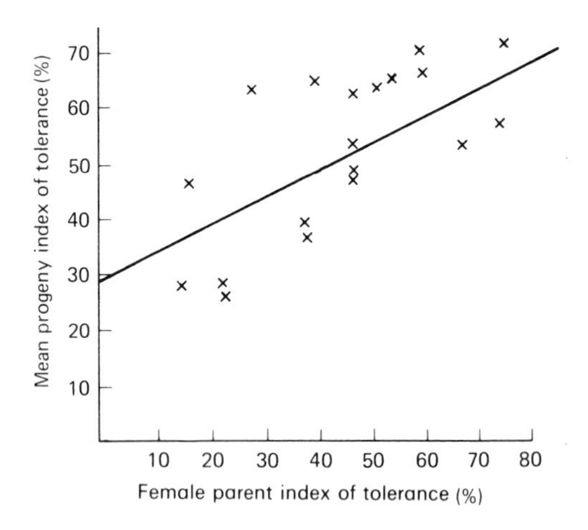

Fig. 5–2 Regression of mean progeny index of zinc tolerance on female parent zinc tolerance in tufted hair grass from Minera zinc mine: the regression coefficient is equal to half the narrow sense heritability so that the heritability of zinc tolerance in this material is very high. ($y = 0.59x + 26.1$)

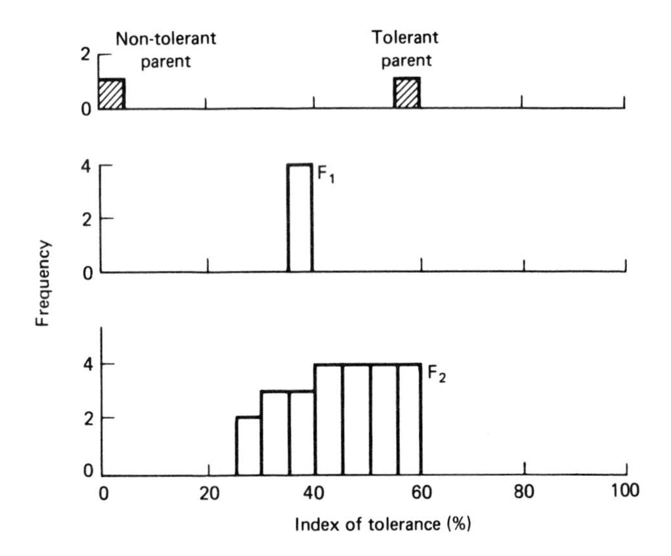

Fig. 5–3 Histograms of index of tolerance for a pair cross between zinc tolerant and non tolerant plants of sweet vernal grass. Segregation in the F_2 generation suggests polygenic control of tolerance, with tolerance showing a degree of dominance (GARTSIDE and MCNEILLY, 1974a).

Parent/progeny regression techniques do not provide us with much information about whether or not major genes are involved in the control of characters. This can only be assessed by examining the segregation pattern of progenies of controlled crosses. This has been done in several species. Figure 5–3 shows the results obtained for sweet vernal grass (*Anthoxanthum odoratum*), which are similar to those for other species. The continuous variation in the F_2 indicates that the character is clearly determined by polygenes and that there is some dominance since the offspring are more similar to the tolerant parent. However in the monkey flower (*Mimulus guttatus*) it seems possible that copper tolerance is controlled by just two pairs of genes.

In sheep's fescue (*Festuca ovina*) the picture is much more complex, since the degree of dominance for tolerance, and indeed whether tolerance or non tolerance is dominant, varies in different crosses. It was suggested a long time ago by Fisher that characters being selected for strongly, should show dominance. Metal tolerance fits this hypothesis. Sheep's fescue, then, is perhaps a situation in which the evolution of dominance has not yet progressed far.

5.3 Conclusion

What then can we conclude about the genetic basis of heavy metal tolerance? It seems that in general the character is very much like that of other important complex characters such as yield in crop plants or height in humans. It is determined by many genes, usually with small effect (i.e. polygenes), not of necessity related to other characters. It has a high narrow sense heritability, suggesting that a rapid response to selection for the character would be expected. This is due to the significant additive genetic component controlling variation in tolerance.

Because there is also a significant dominance component controlling variation in tolerance, crosses between parents which are tolerant and those which are not tolerant will produce progeny whose mean tolerance tends to be closer to that of the tolerant parent. Crosses between tolerant parents will tend in the main to produce predominantly tolerant progeny. These factors are important in maintaining tolerant populations on toxic soils especially when those populations are small, on mines of small area.

6 Natural Selection in Action

6.1 The origins of tolerance

In evolution every character must have a beginning. Over the long passage of time the ultimate origin of new characters is from gene mutation, changes in the genes themselves. It is usually a process which is difficult to observe because one can never be certain whether a mutation has just occurred or has been present in a population for some time. A good example of evolutionary change where we can be more or less certain that mutations were involved is in warfarin resistance in rats. Resistance suddenly appeared separately in populations in Glasgow, Norway and Wales; this must be due to chance mutations (BERRY, 1977); but such detailed information is not usually available.

Metal-tolerant populations must have had their origins from normal populations which had never experienced metal toxicity and were not tolerant. We can simulate their probable origin by sowing seeds of a normal population of bent grass (*Agrostis tenuis*) on copper mine waste

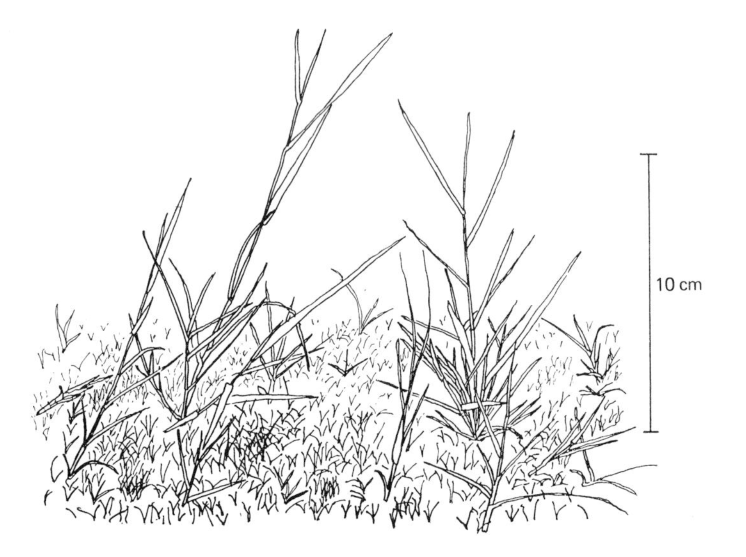

Fig. 6–1 The growth of seedlings of a normal non-tolerant population of bent grass on copper mine soil, slightly ameliorated, after 6 months: nearly all seedlings die, but about 4 in 1000 survive (WALLEY *et al.*, 1974).

ameliorated slightly with garden soil and watered carefully. They all grow well to begin with; soon, however, the seedlings start dying – they have no roots – until after 4–6 months almost all are dead. But a few, about 4 in 1000, continue growing, some better than others (Fig. 6–1). The distribution of height in this population is very skewed: the dead and dying are the large number below 30 mm, the living are the few above (Fig. 6–2). If we take the survivors and grow them on normal soil and then test their tolerance to copper, we find they are tolerant: some are almost as tolerant as typical mine plants and the tallest seedlings are in fact the most tolerant (Fig. 6–3).

If we carry out this selection experiment with seeds from a population which is already tolerant to another metal, we can get individuals which are tolerant to two metals (Table 7). However if we try to select a normal population for tolerance to two metals at once, by growing them on a mixture of two different mine soils containing, for instance, copper and zinc, we do not usually find survivors. This is almost certainly because the chance of finding the two tolerances combined in the same individual are so small as to be undetectable except in an experiment screening many thousands of individuals.

Of course, as we argued in Chapter 5, we must be certain that tolerance in these individuals is inherited. Normal parent/offspring

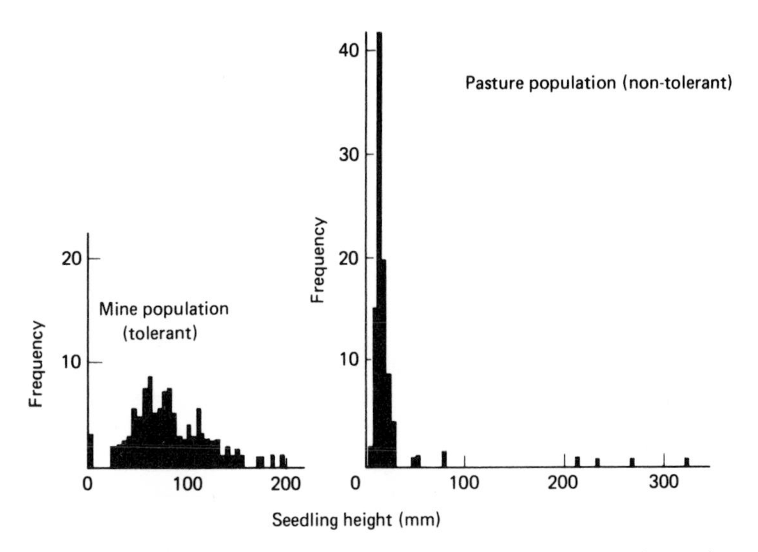

Fig. 6–2 Frequency distribution of height of seedlings of non-tolerant bent grass, compared with tolerant, after growth on slightly ameliorated copper waste for a period of 4 months: seedlings more than 30 mm are survivors (WALLEY *et al.*, 1974).

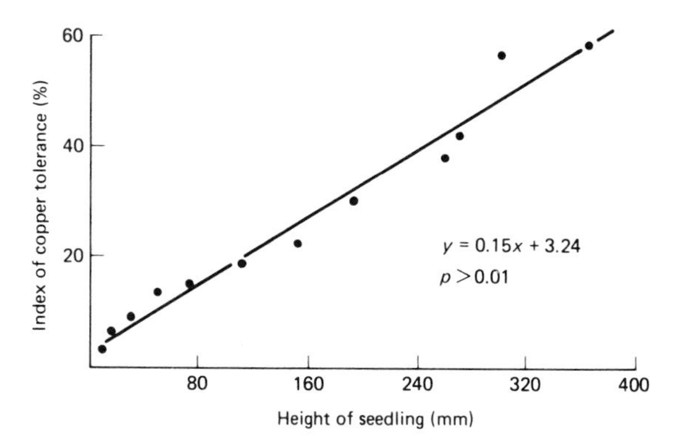

Fig. 6–3 The copper tolerance of seedlings of different height from a normal population after 4 months' growth on slightly ameliorated copper waste: the tall survivors show excellent tolerance, and there is a very close relationship between tolerance and height (WALLEY *et al.*, 1974).

Table 7 Zinc and copper tolerance of survivors from screening normal and copper mine populations on zinc soil compared with other material: the survivors from the copper mine population are now both zinc and copper tolerant (WALLEY *et al.*, 1974).

		Tolerance	
	Individual	*Zinc*	*Copper*
Normal population selected	1	28.6	0.9
(survivors from various	2	41.3	0.0
zinc waste/soil mixtures)	3	25.6	0.0
Copper mine population selected	1	47.8	49.9
(survivors from various zinc	2	30.8	66.9
waste/soil mixtures)	3	30.7	43.5
Pasture population	1	0.0	8.6
(individuals from a pasture)	2	1.7	0.0
	3	0.0	0.0
Copper mine population unselected	1	20.2	76.1
(seed grown on normal soil)	2	16.2	93.5
	3	17.2	86.5
Copper mine population (individual from a mine)	1	0.8	87.5
Zinc mine population (individual from a mine)	1	93.0	3.8
l.s.d. (5% prob.) 7.1			

correlations show that it is. So the raw material on which natural selection can act is in normal populations, and we have the possibility of obtaining a metal tolerant population in not more than one or two generations. Does it happen like this in natural conditions?

6.2 Rapid evolution in nature

Between Liverpool and Manchester, at Prescot, there is a large and successful copper refinery. One cost of success is that it has spread large amounts of copper into the neighbouring areas. Although copper does not harm human beings it is very deleterious to plants, and there is little vegetation in the immediate vicinity of the factory (Fig. 6–4). However in this region there is a series of lawns of different ages established in an attempt to beautify the factory area. Surprisingly, there are some very good lawns on some of the most polluted soils. The reason is not far to seek: a simple rooting test for copper tolerance shows that it is because they are made up of tolerant individuals, mainly of creeping bent grass (*Agrostis stolonifera*). When the site was investigated these lawns could not have been more than 70 years old, because the factory did not exist before this. So the evolution could not have taken more than 70 years.

Some of the lawns, often growing rather poorly, are much younger, however. It turns out that they are made up of less tolerant populations. A survey by Wu shows that there is an evolutionary time series (Fig. 6–5). What is exciting is that tolerance is even to be found in lawns which are four years old. Allowing for difficulties of establishment in natural conditions this means that the rate of evolution is not so different to the rate occurring in a box experiment.

Normal populations of creeping bent grass contain a very low frequency of tolerant individuals, but sown on the contaminated refinery soils these are the only individuals that survive. Selection occurs first, therefore, at the seedling stage and young 'lawns' around the refinery consist of isolated individuals (Fig. 6–6). However in these 'lawns' the individuals are of different sizes. It turns out that the larger

Fig. 6–4 The effects of copper pollution on the railway cutting at Prescot, Lancashire. (**a**) Close to the refinery and (**b**) 1 km away: over 70 years the pollution has eliminated everything but species able to evolve tolerance.

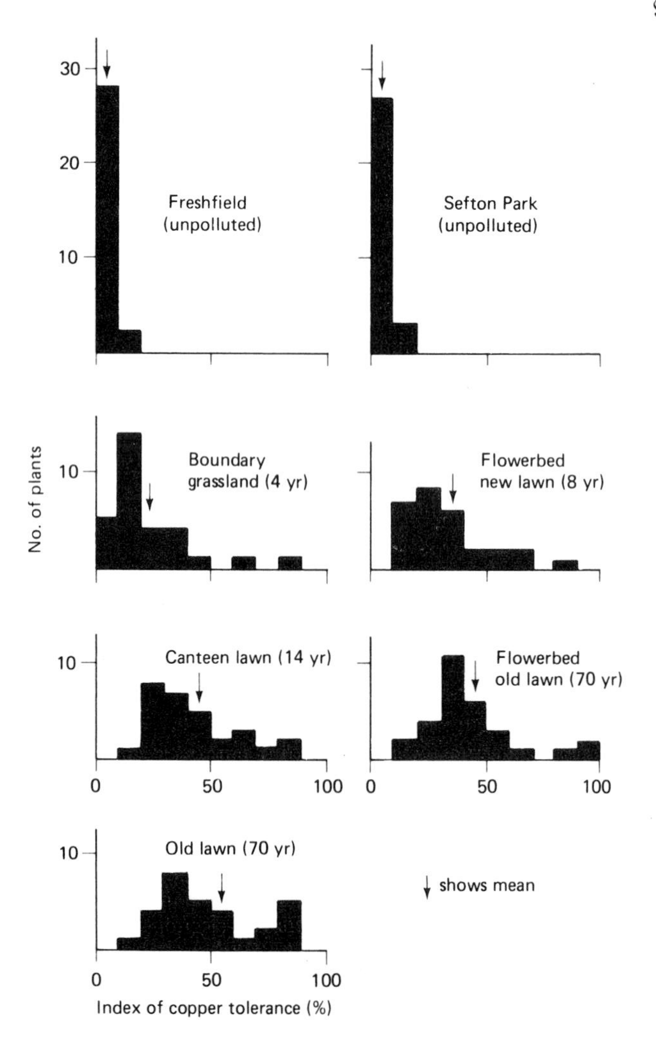

Fig. 6–5 The distribution of copper tolerance in populations of different ages around a copper refinery near Liverpool. Arrows indicate mean values: they form an evolutionary series (WU *et al.*, 1975).

individuals are more tolerant than smaller individuals. So selection is also occurring among the adults, a possibility that is often forgotten.

How many individuals ultimately survive to make up a lawn? It is possible that the old lawns might consist of just a few superior individuals which have spread vegetatively. By a careful test for this, analysing protein differences by gel electrophoresis, Wu showed that a lawn of about $100\,m^2$ contains at least 100 separate individual

Fig. 6–6 Part of a lawn sown with commercial bent grass in 1973 at the Prescot copper refinery; the patchiness is the result of selection eliminating all but copper-tolerant individuals which are now developing into a new population.

genotypes. So the populations have not yet been constrained by selection to a small number of individuals. This has important evolutionary implications, since small numbers of founders can give rise to special characteristics of a population by chance (founder effect) rather than as a product of natural selection. The changes at Prescot are undoubtedly due to selection.

6.3 Evolution of the hulls of ships

What has happened at Prescot could be unique; but all the arguments about evolution we have used so far suggest that this is unlikely. It is fascinating therefore to see what is occurring on the hulls of ocean-going ships.

The underwater part of a newly launched ship is an extensive, vacant, uncolonized habitat for marine organisms. Little wonder then that it becomes rapidly colonized by marine plants and animals, especially algae and barnacles. They project into the water flowing over the hull surface, and substantially increase the resistance to the passage of the hull through the water. A badly fouled ship can require 10% more energy, and therefore fuel, to move it. This colonization has to be prevented.

In the days of wooden ships it was found that copper provided the answer. If the underwater part of the ship was completely sheathed in copper, fouling was considerably reduced. Nowadays hulls are painted with copper-containing antifouling paints which are formulated to release copper slowly into the water to prevent plant and animal colonization.

These reduce fouling considerably. Nevertheless after a time hulls become covered with algae, *Ectocarpus siliculosus* especially, although the paint still contains and is releasing copper. The reason for this can be found by comparing the growth, in different levels of copper, of ship-fouling *Ectocarpus* with that of samples of the same species collected from an unpolluted shore (it is a common shore plant) (Fig. 6–7). RUSSELL and MORRIS (1970) showed that the populations coming from two ships docking in Liverpool can tolerate ten times the concentration tolerated by the population from Anglesey. This tolerance must develop as a result of evolutionary processes.

About once a year a ship is cleaned and repainted. So these tolerant populations must evolve anew every time unless they can come from other populations when ships are side by side in harbour. Just as in bent grass, there appears to be a very low frequency of tolerant individuals in normal populations. Once a few of these colonies settle on the ship they can complete the colonization by the rapid production of asexual zoospores which swim and then settle to give rise to new plants.

6.4 The control exercised by variability

All this suggests that natural selection can easily create an adapted population. But this is true only if the necessary variability is present in

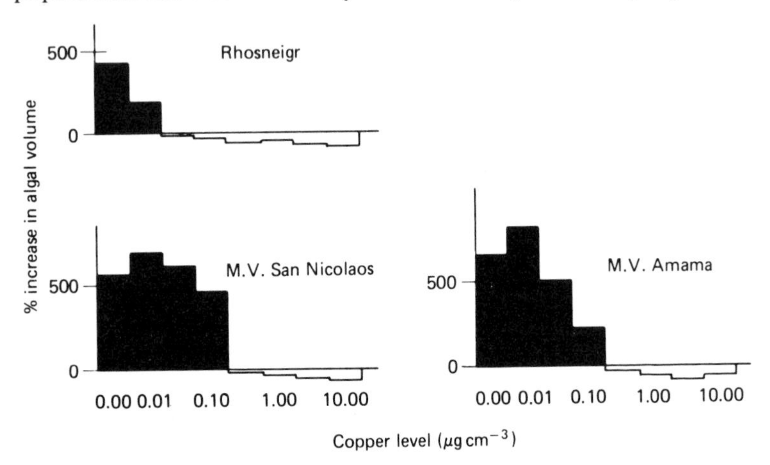

Fig. 6–7 The growth, at different copper levels, of populations of *Ectocarpus siliculosus* from the hulls of two ships and from Rhosneigr, an unpolluted environment. The ship populations can withstand 10 × greater copper concentration than the normal population (RUSSEL and MORRIS, 1970; by permission of *Nature*, Macmillan Journals Ltd).

Table 8 Species to be found in mown grassland in copper contaminated and uncontaminated areas at Prescot, Lancashire (BRADSHAW, 1976).

Species found in mown grasslands at Prescot on soils containing > 2000 pm Cu		
Agrostis stolonifera		*Festuca rubra*
Agrostis tenuis		*Agropyron repens*
Species commonly found in mown grasslands near Prescot on soils containing < 500 ppm Cu (apart from those above)		
Ranunculus repens	*Plantago lanceolata*	*Poa annua*
Ranunculus bulbosus	*Bellis perennis*	*Poa pratensis*
Cerastium vulgatum	*Achillea millefolium*	*Poa trivialis*
Trifolium repens	*Hypochaeris radicata*	*Dactylis glomerata*
Trifolium pratense	*Leontodon autumnale*	*Cynosurus cristatus*
Taraxacum officinale	*Luzula campestris*	*Hordeum murinum*
Rumex obtusifolius	*Lolium perenne*	*Holcus lanatus*
Prunella vulgaris		

the original population. Without genetically based variability, natural selection cannot have any evolutionary effect.

If we go back to any metal contaminated area a striking fact emerges; compared with the surrounding vegetation, the contaminated area has very few species on it (Table 8). There appear to be many species that are not able to evolve tolerance. This cannot be for lack of natural selection, because they will have been present in the vicinity, scattering their seeds on the contaminated area, for as long as the successful species. It must be because of lack of suitable variability.

An easy way to check this is to screen the seed of normal populations of these species for presence of tolerant individuals. Gartside found that they do not contain any seed that gives rise to fully tolerant survivors and certainly not tolerant offspring (Table 9). When this table was published the performance of cocksfoot (*Dactylis glomerata*) was an enigma for here was a species not found on mines which did contain tolerant individuals. Tolerant populations of it have now been found growing on a base rich copper mine in Wales. It is probably normally excluded from copper mine soils because of their low nutrient content rather than their copper toxicity.

These findings are tremendously important, because it is easy to forget that, in the end, it is the supply of genetically-based variability which controls evolution. If more genetic variability was available more evolution would be possible. This is why plant breeders spend a great deal of time hybridizing species to bring together genes from different backgrounds, and searching for distant wild and primitive cultivated materials in case they contain genes not present in normal material.

6.5 Natural selection and fitness

Fitness, from a biological point of view, is the ability to leave descendants. It is usually thought of in relative terms – one species,

Table 9 Variability in copper tolerance available for selection in different grass species determined by screening normal populations by growth on mine soils (GARTSIDE and McNEILLY, 1974b and personal communication).

	Survivors per 5000 plants		*Copper tolerance (%)*		
Species	*on mine soil*	*on ameliorated mine soil*	*five best survivors*	*five best offspring*	*unselected material*
Found on copper waste					
Agrostis tenuis	2	4	55	35	6
Not found on copper waste					
Arrhenatherum elatius	0	4	8	6	0
Poa trivialis	0	2	5		0
Cynosurus cristatus	0	2	6		0
Lolium perenne	0	5	11	9	0
*Dactylis glomerata**	0	6	48	43	5

* Now known to grow on copper waste.

genotype or individual is compared with another – because it is difficult to set absolute values of fitness. A real measure of fitness can only be obtained from a study of the number of surviving offspring, but we sometimes measure just seed output, or, in perennial grasses, plant size, because these are closely related to the ability to leave descendants.

Selection is the complement of fitness, since when selection acts to eliminate an individual or a genotype from a population, it does so to the extent that the individual or genotype is not fit. So if we look at fitnesses we can see how selection acts.

On toxic, metal contaminated, soils non-tolerant individuals from normal populations are considerably less fit than individuals possessing tolerance. In most metal contaminated environments non-tolerant individuals die; so selection against them is 100%. This explains why evolution of metal tolerance can occur so rapidly: the graph of change in gene frequency given in Fig. 1–3 is a pale shadow of what actually happens. Yet, of course, in some metal-contaminated habitats where metal levels are not so high, selection may not be so extreme. This probably explains why non-tolerant individuals still occur in the populations at Prescot (Fig. 6–5).

What happens on normal soils? Does the reverse occur, so that selection against tolerant individuals is 100%? In fact, no: there is never any sign of this, for we can always grow metal-tolerant individuals on normal soils. Often they grow almost as well as normal individuals, and it can be very difficult to find any difference in fitness between normal and copper-tolerant bent grass (*Agrostis tenuis*) when grown as spaced plants in normal soil. But the situation is quite different when the plants are grown in competition with other plants. Now, metal-tolerant plants are relatively less fit than normal plants, and the effects of this accumulate with the passage of time (Fig. 6–8). So metal tolerance does

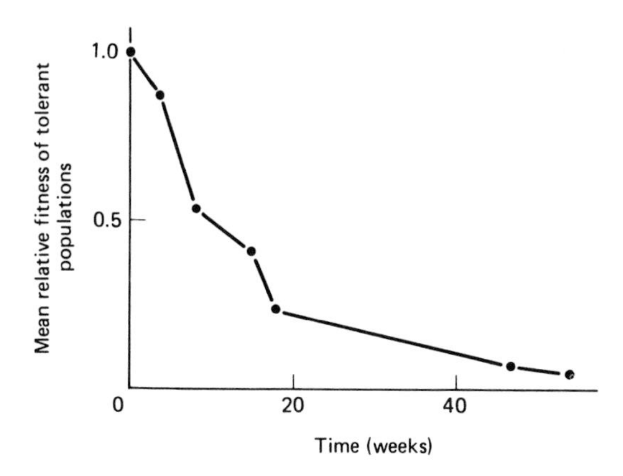

Fig. 6–8 The reduction in mean relative fitness with time of metal-tolerant populations of four species (*Agrostis tenuis*, *Anthoxanthum odoratum*, *Plantago lanceolata* and *Rumex acetosa*), in competition with *Lolium perenne*. Relative fitness is measured as growth of tolerant population in competition/growth of non-tolerant population in competition. The fitness of tolerant individuals falls to a low level very quickly. (HICKEY and McNEILLY, 1975).

appear to cost plants something and to weaken their fitness in normal, competitive, situations.

It does not seem unreasonable that the metal tolerance mechanism should weaken the plant a little. A barrier to free movement of metal within the plant could well make the plant deficient in that metal when only a low external concentration is available. In several cases metal tolerant plants have been found to grow better in metal concentrations slightly above normal: in other words they are not fully fit in normal soils. Zinc-tolerant thrift (*Armeria maritima*) and sweet vernal grass (*Anthoxanthum odoratum*) show this to a marked extent.

So we arrive at a situation when we can see that selection can work in two directions. It favours tolerant individuals very strongly on toxic soils, which explains the rapid evolution of metal-tolerant populations: and it favours non-tolerant individuals on normal soils (although not so strongly). This should keep genes for tolerance out of normal populations: the significance of this will appear when we look at the pattern of evolution in the field.

7 Patterns of Evolution and the Effects of Migration

7.1 Evolution over short distances

Mining for heavy metals reached its peak development in the United Kingdom between 1780 and 1880, and hence much of the toxic mine spoils which litter old mining districts are 100–200 years old, although some may be much older. As we have seen at Prescot the evolution of tolerant populations is a rapid process, and we can assume that tolerant plants would have begun colonization of mine spoils soon after they appeared, leading to the evolution of metal-tolerant populations.

In view of their age it might reasonably be expected that some colonization of adjacent normal soils by metal-tolerant plants would have taken place, and a gradual change, or *cline*, from full tolerance on the mine to uniform non-tolerance on normal soil would have developed. Such a pattern should be revealed by examining the distribution of tolerance across the boundary between toxic mine soil and normal pasture soil. Figure 7–1 shows the pattern for zinc tolerance at the boundary of a small zinc mine at Trelogan in North Wales. The situation is quite a remarkable one, because the frequency of metal-tolerant individuals changes abruptly over a distance of just a few metres between sites 4 and 5, the mine supporting exclusively tolerant individuals, the pasture exclusively non-tolerants. Selection must be operating in completely opposite directions in the two habitats – reflecting the selection pressures outlined in Chapter 6 which operate on toxic and normal soils.

There is however a factor which we must not overlook, which opposes natural selection, caused by the processes which disperse genes in space through the movement of adults, seeds or gametes. It is termed *gene flow*.

7.2 Patterns of gene flow

The seeds of plants are usually light and easily dispersed but it is the microscopic pollen grains carried by wind or insects which are the most easily dispersed. So where mine and non-mine populations come into contact with each other, as at a mine edge, gene flow comes about mainly as a result of pollen interchange between them. This raises three important questions; how far is pollen transported, what is the pattern

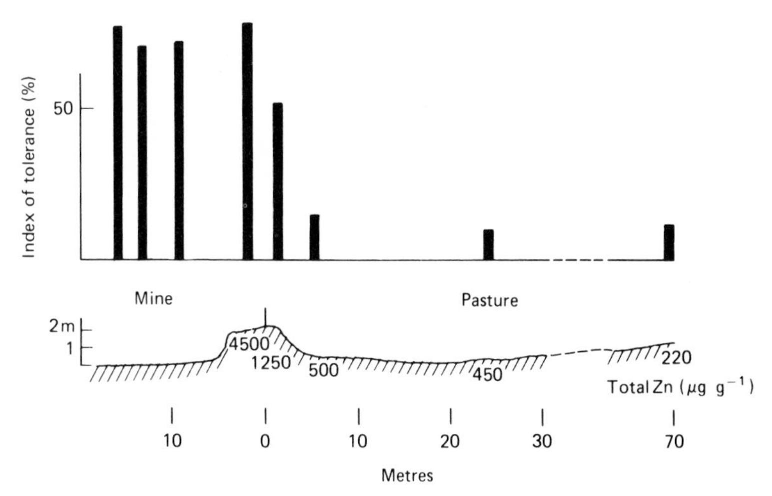

Fig. 7–1 The distribution of zinc tolerance in populations of sweet vernal grass along a transect from mine to pasture at Trelogan mine, North Wales. There is a sharp demarcation between tolerant populations on the mine and normal populations on the pasture (Putwain in JAIN and BRADSHAW, 1966).

of pollen transport, and consequently what effect does gene flow have on patterns of evolution?

Pollen dispersal and gene flow have been examined in plants by several workers. Obviously in any wind pollinated species pollen distribution from a source is markedly influenced by wind direction, being carried strongly downwind. What is less obvious is that although pollen can be blown hundreds of miles, the bulk of pollen transport occurs over very short distances. In spaced plants of ryegrass, (*Lolium perenne*) the amount of gene flow from a genetically marked source was found to be as little as 5% over 10m (Fig. 7–2). In a continuous sward the amount of gene flow was found to be much smaller, negligible at 6 m and undetectable at 12 m. The same sort of values are found in insect-pollinated plants, because bees and other pollinators do not on average move very far.

Gene flow can take place then, but what evidence do we have for gene flow in nature? We can test for it very easily by comparing population samples derived from seed produced by a group of plants flowering in field conditions, which could be affected by gene flow, and from that same group of plants flowering in isolation in, say, a greenhouse. Differences in the characteristics of the seed produced will reflect the amount of gene flow. The data given in Fig. 7–3 are from such an experiment for a copper-tolerant population at the copper mine at Drws-y-Coed, North Wales. Clearly gene flow does occur, bringing non-

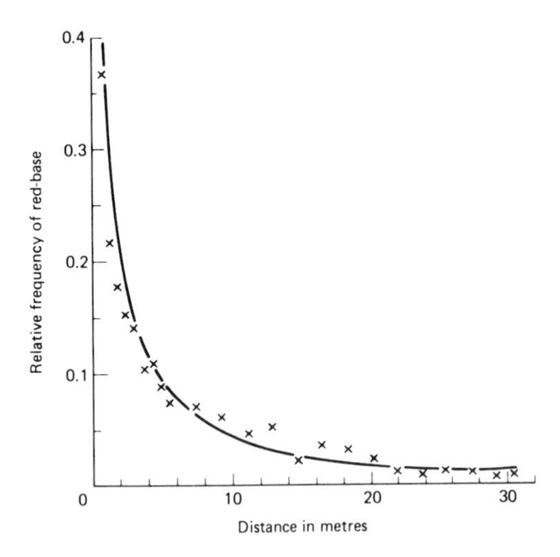

Fig. 7–2 The pattern of pollen movement and hence gene flow in perennial ryegrass, as spaced plants: the data represent the frequency of occurrence of red tiller-base (simple dominant) in seed produced by white tiller-based (simple recessive) ryegrass arranged in a regular pattern downwind from a block of red-based plants (GLEAVES, 1975).

adapted genes for non-tolerance into the tolerant mine population. In spite of the gene flow, however, the mine population is able to maintain high tolerance, which must be due to continuing high selection pressure favouring tolerance. In such a situation the selection overcomes the opposing force of gene flow, in spite of considerable gene flow.

We know from Chapter 6 that selection on normal soil against tolerant individuals is less strong than that promoting tolerance on toxic soils. Is it possible to find a situation where a non-tolerant population is subjected to high gene flow from a tolerant population, and again examine the balance between selection and gene flow? Perhaps gene flow might overcome selection. The mine at Drws-y-Coed provides an excellent example. The mine is shown in Fig. 7–4. It is a small mine in a steep sided glaciated valley which runs from east to west. The whole area is covered with grassland containing bent grass (*Agrostis tenuis*). The mine carries a population of tolerant bent grass, but is surrounded by normal non-tolerant populations. The prevailing winds are from the west, blowing up the valley. They carry predominantly non-tolerant pollen into the mine from the non-tolerant populations upwind of the mine as we saw in Fig. 7–3. But they must also carry predominantly tolerant pollen from the mine into the populations downwind from the mine. So two transects were taken, one upwind from toxic mine soil for

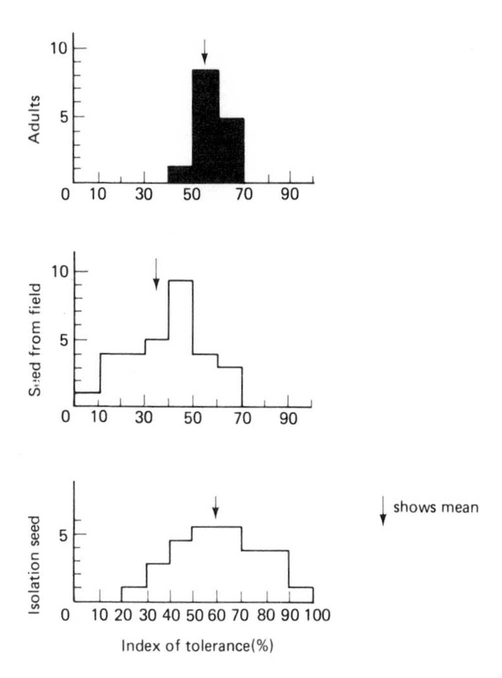

Fig. 7–3 The copper tolerances of adult plants of bent grass from Drws-y-Coed mine, Gwynedd, and seed produced by them in the field, and in isolation: the difference between field and isolation seed reflects the considerable gene flow into the adult population.

10 m into the adjacent uncontaminated soil, the other taken downwind out into the uncontaminated soil for 150 m.

There is clearly a striking difference between the tolerance of the adult populations along these two transects (Fig. 7–5). Whereas tolerant individuals disappear after just 1 m on normal soil in the upwind direction, in the downwind direction at least some tolerant plants survive on normal soil as much as 180 m from the mine boundary. When we look at the tolerance of the seed produced by these plants in the field, the reason for this difference becomes apparent. In the upwind direction very little gene flow is occurring out from the mine, so that the tolerance of the seed generation follows very closely that of the adults. By contrast in the downwind direction there is considerable gene flow out from the mine, so that the tolerance of the seed generation is greater on average than that of the adult plants.

Here is a situation in which gene flow is highly polarized. There is considerable gene flow into the mine population tending to dilute tolerance but the tolerance of the population is maintained, since

Fig. 7–4 View of the copper mine at Drws-y-Coed, Gwynedd: genes for non tolerance are carried into the mine, and genes for tolerance out of the mine, by the movement of pollen in the prevailing wind, the direction of which is shown by the wind-blown hawthorn in the foreground (photograph by A. J. Tollitt).

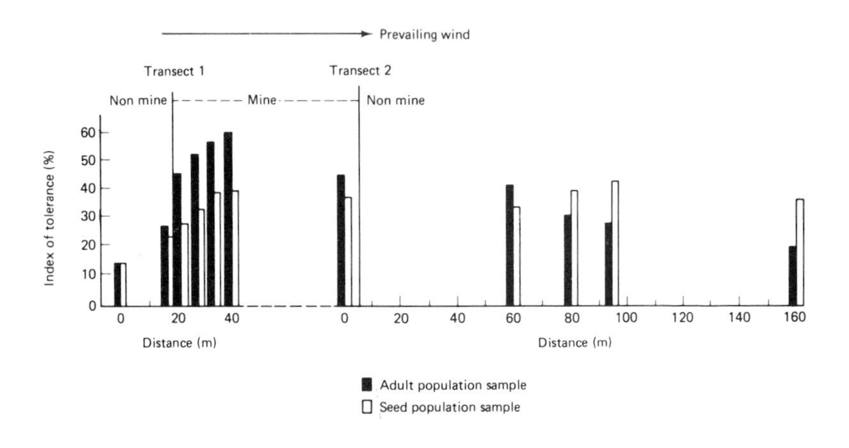

Fig. 7–5 Copper tolerance in adult and naturally produced seed populations of bent grass at Drws-y-Coed copper mine: there is considerable interaction of gene flow and selection (McNEILLY, 1968).

selection on the mine for tolerance is also considerable and overcomes the effects of gene flow. On normal soil selection is not so strong. With low gene flow in the upwind direction the non tolerance of the pasture populations is maintained. With high gene flow in the downwind direction from the mine plants to the normal, pasture plants, selection is unable to maintain the non tolerance of the pasture population. So evolutionary divergence of the populations here is prevented.

7.3 Models of gene flow

All this seems to make sense from an intuitive point of view. But some people find it difficult to believe that the evolutionary differentiation of adjacent populations can take place on such a localized scale, because they cannot believe that gene flow can so easily be held in check by selection (except in cases where gene flow is strong and selection weak).

It is very easy to set up a model of what would happen on a computer. A series of populations can be envisaged in a line across an environmental boundary, so that in half of them selection is in favour of a gene and in the other half selection is against the gene. The populations can be simulated on the computer, each starting as a mixture of gene A and its allele gene a, and can be made to reproduce, grow and suffer selection so that individuals containing gene A are either favoured or disfavoured. At the same time, when at each generation each population reproduces, it can be arranged that gene flow occurs, so that neighbouring populations receive some genes from the population being allowed to reproduce. This has to be done for each population, for each generation, and would be almost impossible to work out mathematically: but on a computer each generation can be calculated in a fraction of a second, and the whole history of what happens over a large number of generations until an equilibrium is reached, can be worked out in a few minutes.

If the sort of gene flow that has been observed in grasses (Fig. 7–2) is assumed, the resulting patterns of evolutionary differentiation among ten populations is shown in Fig. 7–6. When selection for and against gene A is not very strong, the change at the boundary is not very sharp although it does occur. When selection is stronger, similar to what we think is occurring in the field, the change between the populations on the two sides of the environmental boundaries is very abrupt indeed, just as at Trelogan. If we put into the model polarized gene flow as at Drws-y-Coed we can get results which resemble closely that which occurs in practice.

So these striking differences between populations only a short distance apart can be explained theoretically. It means that we can expect evolution of a local adapted population even in a very small area, a few metres across, if selection is strong enough. People are now finding

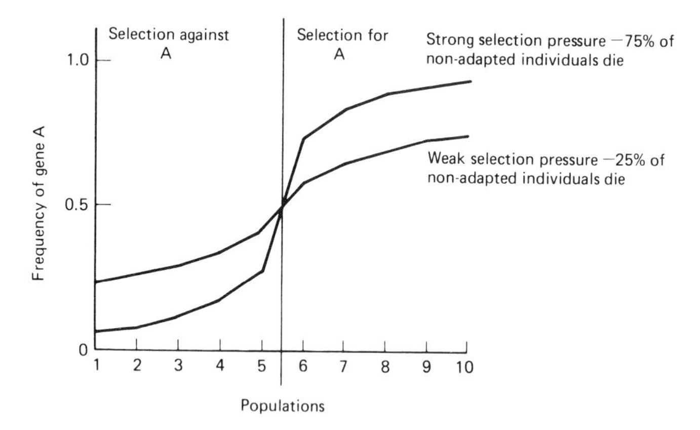

Fig. 7–6 The results of simulating the interaction between gene flow and selection in a series of populations across an environmental boundary on a computer: every generation there is gene flow between populations but selection is against gene A in populations 1–5, and in favour of it in populations 6–10. The result is a cline which is very steep when selection is high. Equivalent natural spacing of populations 4 m (JAIN and BRADSHAW, 1966).

evolution of zinc tolerance occurring even in the foot wide strip of land which gets polluted by zinc under a galvanized, zinc coated, fence and on piles of mine waste a few metres in diameter.

7.4 Barriers to gene flow

Some of the products of gene flow into the mine population are, as we see from Fig. 7–3, non-tolerant individuals, not adapted for survival on mine soil. This is a waste of the resources of the mine plants, particularly those at the edge of the mine which are subject to the greatest gene flow because of the pattern of pollen movement. In such a situation the reproductive fitness – the ability to produce viable descendants – of mine edge plants would be enhanced by any mechanism which reduced gene flow, i.e. the development of *breeding barriers* between adjacent populations.

In plants, one of the simplest methods for reducing cross pollination and hence gene flow between populations is through the development of differences in flowering time. There are many instances where differences in flowering time have been recorded for ecotypes within a species or between closely-related species. As far as metal-tolerant races are concerned several of the early workers found that lead mine races of bent grass (*Agrostis tenuis*) flower from four days to one week earlier than adjacent pasture populations. In bladder campion (*Silene inflata*) BROKER (1963) found that zinc-tolerant individuals flowered on average several weeks earlier than normal individuals.

More detailed evidence is available for flowering time for copper-tolerant populations of bent grass and zinc-tolerant populations of sweet vernal grass (*Anthoxanthum odoratum*). The flowering time in the field along transects from mine to pasture for bent grass at Drws-y-Coed mine in North Wales are given in Fig. 7–7. Plants which occur at the edges of the mine flower earlier than adjacent pasture populations, by some six to eight days. Such a difference in flowering time would cause a reduction in gene flow and a consequent increase in reproductive fitness.

This information is, however, taken from plants in the field. The differences that were found may simply be caused by differences in the environments in which the plants grew. However when the plants are taken into cultivation, differences in flowering time are maintained, the mine edge plants again flowering earlier than plants from mine middle or

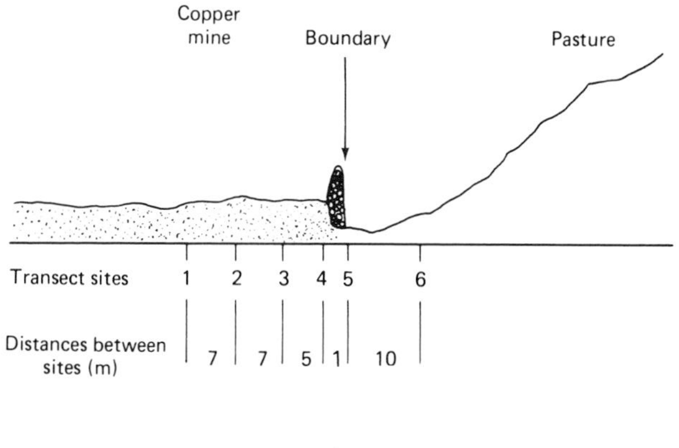

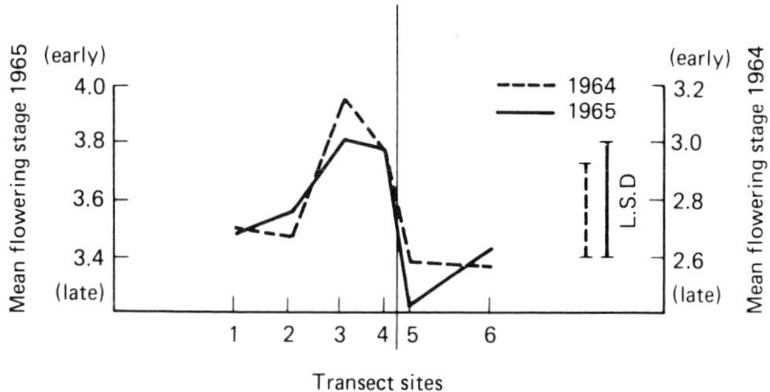

Fig. 7–7 Flowering time in bent grass along a transect from mine to pasture at Drws-y-Coed mine: Plants at the mine edge flower much earlier than those from the adjacent pasture, restricting gene flow between them (McNEILLY and ANTONOVICS, 1968).

from the pasture. The genetic basis of flowering time differences in bent grass from Drws-y-Coed have been analysed: there are additive genetic effects. This all suggests that early flowering in mine edge populations is due to selection for earliness of flowering. If this were the case, it would be expected that under strong stabilizing selection the variance of populations would be reduced, whilst less strong selection would lead to increased variance. An examination of coefficients of variation in the sub populations at Drws-y-Coed shows that the mine edge populations, 3 and 4, have markedly reduced variation when compared with either mine middle or non mine populations.

Site No.	1	2	3	4	5	6
Coefficient of variation for flowering time	0.0116	0.0056	0.0042	0.0082	0.0104	0.0150

This suggests that early flowering in mine edge populations is the product of quite strong selection pressures.

How would such selection operate? If tolerant plants flower earlier than pasture plants, they will intercross with each other, and their offspring will tend to have a higher overall tolerance than if they had crossed with adjacent non-tolerant plants even though there is some degree of dominance for tolerance as we saw in Chapter 5. They will thus leave more adapted or tolerant offspring which will also carry the genes for early flowering, and the establishment of tolerant and early flowering individuals will be promoted by selection.

7.5 Long distance migration

If we look at the evidence for the way pollen moves given in Fig. 7–2, we can see that, although most pollen only moves a short distance, some pollen goes a very long way – something which hay fever sufferers know well. This should mean that genes can move a long way, not in sufficient quantity to alter the general character of the populations that receive them, but enough to add a low level of variability to the populations.

An excellent example of this occurs in the vicinity of the very large Parys Mountain copper mine at Amlwch on Anglesey, North Wales. M. S. I. Khan collected a number of seed samples from bent grass (*Agrostis tenuis*) populations growing on the mine and at different distances downwind from the mine. He determined the number of tolerant individuals in each of the populations by sowing the seed on toxic mine soil. By this he could estimate how far genes for tolerance could spread from the mine. The results are really quite remarkable (Fig. 7–8). Considerable numbers of tolerant individuals, more than in normal populations, were detected three miles downwind of the mine. This can arise by gene flow, by pollen, directly from the mine itself. But it can also arise from tolerant individuals established downwind of Parys Mountain mine on normal soils as in the downwind transect at Drws-y-Coed. Over a period of years tolerance would, as a result of this process, migrate further and further from the mine. Whichever is the correct explanation, we have excellent evidence for the way genes can move from one population to another over long distances. It is a way in which variability can be maintained in populations. This could be important when populations have to evolve in the future to further pollution, or to any environmental stress.

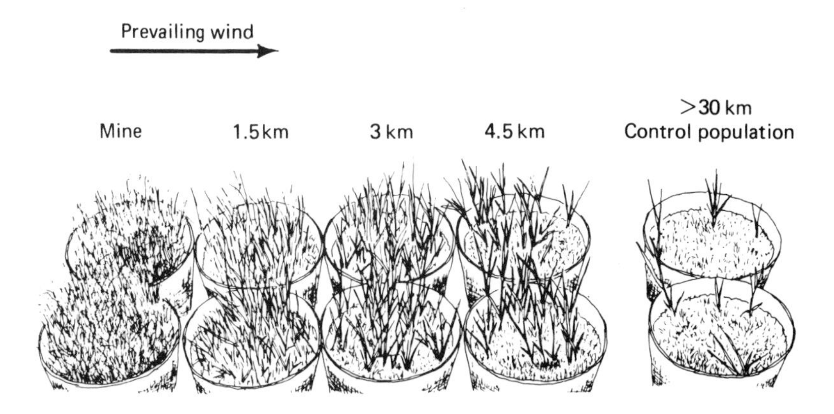

Fig. 7–8 The growth of seedlings taken from normal populations of bent grass a long distance downwind from the large copper mine Parys Mountain. Gene flow maintains a higher number of tolerant individuals than usual even 5 km away from the mine.

8 The Practical Uses of Tolerance and Resistance

8.1 Metal tolerance in land reclamation

The very mine wastes which have given us such an insight into evolution have an unattractive side to them. They are sources of serious heavy metal pollution (Table 5, p. 27) which can affect the surrounding countryside. Very often the material is finely ground, and can blow in the wind or wash away in times of heavy rain. There are innumerable records of crops being damaged and livestock killed in England and Wales. Even as recently as 1964 rich lowland pastures in the Conway Valley in North Wales were ruined when a wash out from the tailings heap at the Parc mine covered 25 ha with a layer of material half a metre deep containing 0.1 % lead and 1 % zinc (Fig. 8–1). In an average soil, levels of lead and zinc higher than 0.05 % (500 p.p.m.) begin to be serious to crops and stock (see Chapter 4).

Fig. 8–1 Erosion of metalliferous tailings at Parc Mine, Gwynedd. A storm carried thousands of tonnes of material onto neighbouring pastures and destroyed them.

Mines for heavy metals are scattered throughout the world. As the rich ore-bodies become exhausted man is having to mine more extensive low grade ore-bodies instead. This means larger operations and larger deposits of waste. Even with modern technology it is impossible to remove all the metal from the ore so the wastes are often very toxic. In Utah, the Kennecott copper mine has a tailings pond 13 km^2 in area which rises by 6 m a year: the total output of waste from the copper mines in the Tucson region of Arizona is one million tonnes yr^{-1}.

Where possible these wastes should be returned to the pits from which they were extracted. But in a deep open pit operation this is usually difficult because the mine has to work progressively to lower levels. So the tailings ponds and waste rock dumps grow, and become potential threats to the environment unless they are properly stabilized (Fig. 8–2). A permanent cover of inert material is the most ideal solution. On this a normal vegetation can be re-established (GEMMELL, 1977; BRADSHAW and CHADWICK, 1980).

But such treatments are expensive, and an exciting new alternative is to use nature's own solution, the metal-tolerant plants themselves (SMITH and BRADSHAW, 1979). A typical waste heap does not naturally have a continuous cover of tolerant plants: they are scattered over it (Fig. 4–1). Is this because metal levels are too high in the bare areas for even tolerant plants to grow? Or could it be that the waste is too poor in

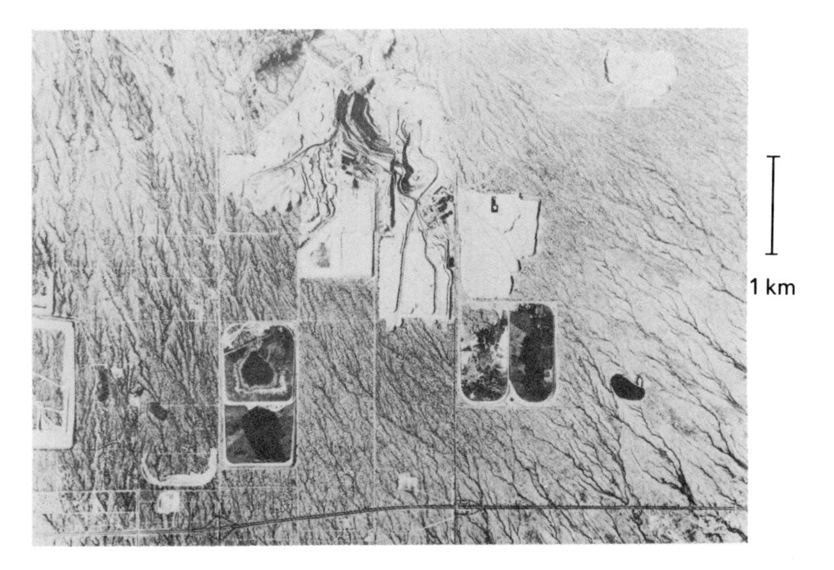

Fig. 8–2 Aerial view of a modern copper mine in Arizona – the open pit is at the top, the rest are waste rock dumps and tailings ponds. Unless properly stabilized these will be a permanent threat to our environment.

plant nutrients? If it was the latter then waste heaps could be covered with metal-tolerant plants if they were given nutrients.

The simplest way to answer this question is to establish an experiment on mine waste comparing the growth of tolerant and non-tolerant populations with and without the addition of nutrients in the form of fertilizer. The results of Rosalind Smith (Fig. 8–3) show the answer very clearly: if fertilizer, especially slow release material, is provided, tolerant populations will grow extremely well: in the absence of fertilizer they will not. Non-tolerant populations show limited growth, but this is only temporary: after two years in this experiment they were all dead.

Local populations can be found on many mines in Britain. Is each adapted only to its own site, or are there populations which do consistently well on all sites? For the calcareous lead/zinc wastes in Britain it appears that the Trelogan population, which comes from wastes high in both lead and zinc, will do consistently well on all calcareous sites (Fig. 8–4).

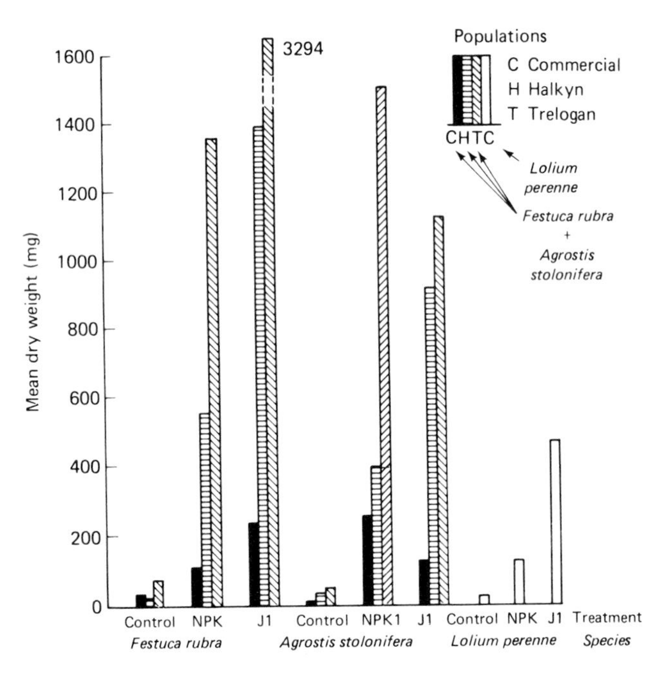

Fig. 8–3 Dry weight of different populations with different fertilizer treatments after seven months' growth on waste at Trelogan mine (NPK, ordinary complete fertilizer, N 120 lb/acre, P 50 lb/acre, K 100 lb/acre; JI, slow-release fertilizer (John Innes base) at equivalent rate). The two tolerant populations. Halkyn and Trelogan are growing well (SMITH and BRADSHAW, 1972).

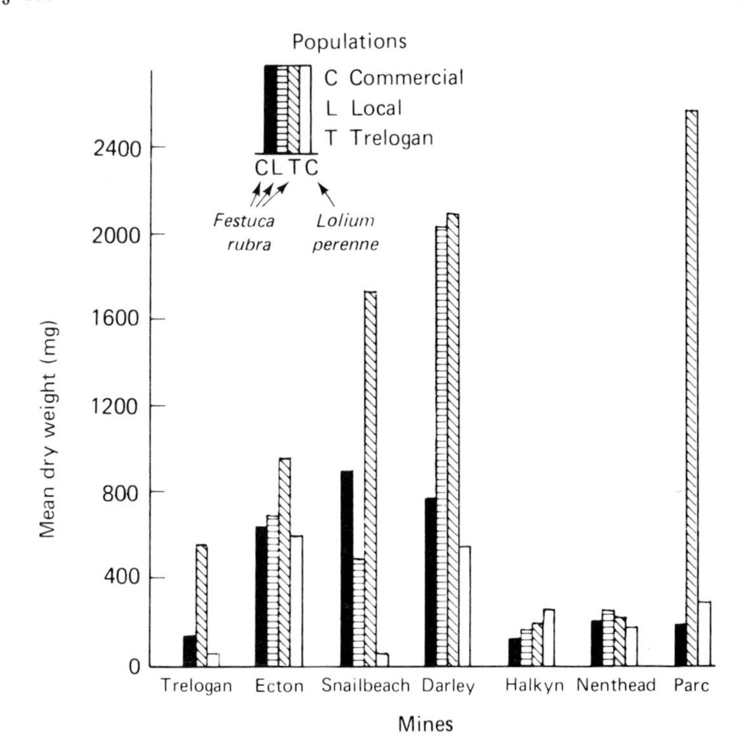

Fig. 8–4 Dry weight of different populations after twelve months' growth on seven different calcareous lead-zinc mines with fertilizer (local population is derived from the site where trial was carried out): the Trelogan population is consistantly the most successful (SMITH and BRADSHAW, 1972).

Once such material has been identified it can be multiplied in large plots on the mine waste. But these can only give limited supplies of seed, so the next step is for further multiplication to be carried out on ordinary soils. There is always the possibility that if there is some variability in tolerance, natural selection will favour non-tolerant genotypes on normal soils, as we have already seen. But this will not be important if the tolerant genotypes themselves grow well on ordinary soil, if the frequency of non-tolerant genotypes is very low, and if the period of seed multiplication is kept to one or, at the most, two generations.

All of these conditions can be complied with, and as a result there are now available for the first time three metal-tolerant varieties of grasses.
Red fescue (*Festuca rubra*) Merlin – calcareous lead/zinc wastes
Bent grass (*Agrostis tenuis*) Goginan – acidic lead/zinc wastes
Bent grass (*Agrostis tenuis*) Parys – copper wastes

Fig. 8–5 A zinc polluted hillside adjoining a smelter at Palmerton, New Jersey sown with zinc-tolerant red fescue, Merlin. The first metal tolerant plant variety grows where everything else has been destroyed by pollution.

Table 10 Analyses of metal contents of different populations growing on lead/zinc waste at Trelogan (total $\mu g\, g^{-1}$ in shoots with or without fertilizer): the tolerant populations contain reduced metal levels but still too high to allow regular grazing by animals (SMITH and BRADSHAW, 1972).

		Lead		*Zinc*	
Species	*Population*	*no fert.*	*with fert.*	*no fert.*	*with fert.*
Agrostis stolonifera	Commercial*	1140	810	2965	1930
	Halkyn	700	454	1783	1310
	Trelogan	462	623	1446	1528
Festuca rubra	Commercial*	2124	495	3854	1915
	Halkyn	102	979	2483	2800
	Trelogan	397	808	1545	1975
Lolium perenne	Commercial†	2293	850	4504	2500

* Plants almost dead.
† Plants died later.

These are beginning to be used to cover and stabilize metal wastes in temperate climates on a world-wide basis (Fig. 8–5). It will be easy to produce varieties for other climates (HUMPHREYS AND BRADSHAW, 1978). Since in a full seasons growth tolerant material does not completely prevent the movement of metals into its foliage (Table 10) the vegetated areas cannot be used for grazing unless animals are only allowed to graze for short periods. But because tolerant material does limit upward movement of metals to a considerable extent it can be of considerable help in the control of pollution.

Mine wastes are not only extreme on account of the metals present, but also, as we saw in Chapter 4, because of low nutrients and physical problems. So it is interesting that these metal-tolerant varieties have been found to be tolerant of low nutrients and drought. This makes them of value for a wide range of difficult habitats besides metal wastes. Part of their adaptation is in slow growth: Merlin is finding use, therefore, as a lawn grass which requires less maintenance.

8.2 Breeding for resistance to air pollution

Ever since we have come to realize the serious damage that air pollution can cause (total damage in U.S.A. in 1968 was $\$16 \times 10^9$; damage to crops in Pennsylvania in 1969 was $\$11.5 \times 10^6$) energetic attempts have been made to reduce it. For plants the main problems are sulphur dioxide and ozone. Sulphur dioxide pollution at ground level can be reduced without too much difficulty by the use of high chimney stacks which disperse the chimney gases more widely and reduce the sulphur concentrations at ground level, or by scrubbers which wash out the sulphur dioxide before it is emitted. But ozone, which is an indirect product of car exhaust fumes, is proving more difficult to control, despite the compulsory use of catalytic converters on car exhausts and other devices. It seems unlikely to disappear as a problem at least in the U.S.A., even with the disappearance of 'gas-guzzling' vehicles, because the number of vehicles continues to increase: and in Europe and elsewhere signs of ozone damage are becoming more common in summer conditions.

In an unfortunate weekend in 1959 growers of cigar wrapper leaf tobacco in Connecticut lost $5 million when the ozone reached very high levels and almost the whole crop was destroyed. The symptoms are a disease known as weather fleck. It was already realized that tobacco varieties differed in their sensitivity to ozone and other oxidants (Fig. 8–6): in fact a variety Bel–W3 is so sensitive that it is now used to assess ozone concentration. Variation has also been found within varieties. So a plant breeding programme involving the hybridization of resistant varieties, and also selection within them, has now produced new ozone resistant varieties, and ozone damage in Connecticut tobacco is becoming a thing of the past.

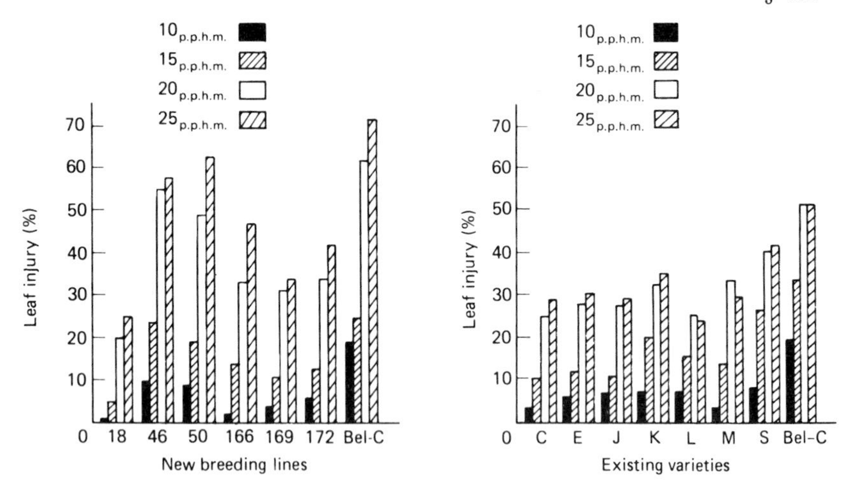

Fig. 8–6 Effects of ozone dosages (varieties p.p.h.m.) on commercial cigar wrapper tobacco developed in Connecticut for weather fleck resistance. The new breeding line 18 has improved resistance over other lines and existing varieties: Bel C is a susceptible control (MENSER and HODGES, 1972).

In other crops ozone damage is common. Where no resistant varieties can be found the crop cannot be grown and whole industries, such as the citrus industry in southern California, have to move elsewhere. Extensive work to identify ozone-resistant varieties is being carried out in many crops: variability seems to be widespread (Table 11). But this is only a beginning, since variation between varieties must occur by accident rather than as the result of positive artificial or natural selection. It is possible to select new breeding lines from variation found within individual varieties (Fig. 8–6) as well as that produced by inter-variety hybridization, to achieve higher levels of resistance, just as in the Illinois corn experiment (Fig. 1–4). Genetic studies of resistance to weather fleck (ozone damage) in tobacco show that it is a character like any other controlled by several genes with additive effects (AYCOCK, 1972). Breeding programmes are under way in beans, onions, and petunias as well as tobacco.

Trees are peculiarly vulnerable to the effects of air pollutants. Sulphur dioxide damage from individual sources has destroyed whole forests. The worst examples are probably at Copper Basin in Tennessee, and in the Sudbury District of Ontario where 1800 km^2 has been severely damaged. But these are localized and high intensity.

It is the widespread pollution of lower concentration which is more serious. Recently a number of conditions of widespread damage, such as chlorotic dwarf, blight, or needle dieback in eastern white pine (*Pinus strobus*) in eastern U.S.A. and chlorotic decline in ponderosa pine (*Pinus ponderosa*) in western U.S.A. have been shown to be due to oxidants

Table 11 Crop, ornamental, and forest species in which variation in sensitivity to pollutants has been observed: resistance to air pollution is not uncommon in economic species (RYDER, 1973).

Species	*Pollutant*
Crop species	
Alfalfa (*Medicago sativa* L.)	Ozone
Citrus (*Citrus* sp.)	Fluoride
Cucumber (*Cucumis sativus* L.)	Ozone
Grain sorghum (*Sorghum vulgare* Pers.)	Fluoride
Green bean (*Phaseolus vulgaris* L.)	Ozone,
Lettuce (*Lactuca sativa* L.)	Ozone
Oats (*Avena sativa* L.)	Ozone
Onion (*Allium cepa* L.)	Ozone
Potato (*Solanum tuberosum* L.)	Ozone
Radish (*Raphanus sativus* L.)	Ozone
Red clover (*Trifolium pratense* L.)	Ozone
Spinach (*Spinacia oleracea* L.)	Oxidant
Sweet corn (*Zea mays* L.)	Oxidant
Tobacco (*Nicotiana tabacum* L.)	Ozone
Tomato (*Lycopersicon esculentum* Mill.)	Ozone
Turfgrass (Several species)	Ozone, SO_2
White bean (*Phaseolus vulgaris* L.)	Oxidant
Ornamental species	
Coleus (*Coleus* sp.)	Ozone
Gladiolus (*Gladiolus* sp.)	Fluoride
Petunia (*Petunia hybrida* Vilm.)	Ozone, PAN, SO_2, NO_2,
Forest species	
Douglas fir (*Pseudotsuga taxifolia* Brit.)	SO_2
Eastern white pine (*Pinus strobus* L.)	Ozone, SO_2
Larch (*Larix* sp.)	SO_2
Lodgepole pine (*Pinus contorta* Dougl.)	SO_2
Norway spruce (*Picea abies* L.)	SO_2, fluoride
Ponderosa pine (*Pinus ponderosa* Laws)	Oxidant, fluoride
Scotch pine (*Pinus sylvestris* L.)	SO_2, fluoride

such as ozone, either alone or in combination with sulphur dioxide.

So far little systematic breeding work has been carried out. But variability in sensitivity to the pollution is very obvious in affected natural populations. So it will not be difficult to establish seed orchards of tolerant individuals. This has been done in white pine in Tennessee.

Breeding for resistance to air pollution is a practical possibility. But air pollutants affect many other things besides plants, including ourselves. So the long term aim must be to reduce pollution. But as a way of overcoming particular problems resistance breeding is important.

9 The Significance of Tolerance

It is easy to think that evolution only takes place in text books – that it is something so slow that it can only be followed in drawings and measurements of a fossil record. Yet it is patently obvious from all that we have described, that it can be very different, a process which can cause major changes in the genetic make up of populations in very few generations. In plants this can mean very few years. So we have to revise our ideas on rates of evolution and the fixity of plant species.

On the other hand selection caused by pollution might appear rather severe and unusual. It is therefore important to realize that similar rapid evolution has been found in plants in relation to other more normal environmental factors. Rapid evolution has even been found in the different fertilizer plots of the Park Grass experiment at Rothamsted Experimental Station (SNAYDON, 1970), and plant breeders now realize that in outbreeding, variable crops they have to watch very carefully for genetic changes occurring as a result of natural selection, undoing all their careful breeding work (see BRADSHAW, 1972).

Evolution is brought to a halt however if the appropriate variability is not present, on which selection can act. Often failure of a species to evolve in adaptation to a new environment can be put down to the competitive effects of other species which prevent it from finding space in the new environment. In the evolution of metal tolerance the new environments are wide open, and failure to evolve tolerance really does seem to be due to lack of the appropriate genetically-based variation.

This means that the ecological amplitude of a species – its ability to enter or persist in new environments – can be controlled not only by its innate physiological flexibility, but also by its capacity to evolve – its genetical flexibility. It has often been suggested that in evolution some species and groups failed to survive because they were not adaptable enough, meaning too specialized. We can now see that it probably means that they did not possess the appropriate genetic variation.

Pollution can occur in small, highly localized areas. In these situations we would once have thought that gene flow from neighbouring populations would have prevented the evolution of new, adapted populations. However all the cases examined show that this is far from true. Adapted populations can be found on piles of waste only a few metres across, or even (to reduce the matter almost to absurdity) under a galvanized wire fence. In the case of the fence the evolution must be the sifting out of adapted genotypes from the local normal population; the selected individuals cannot breed together easily. But an adapted population results. When the populations are more than a few metres in extent they clearly have integrity. Again, pollution might be providing extreme examples, but we now know that highly localized evolution in plants is commonplace in normal kinds of habitats (JAIN and BRADSHAW, 1966).

In the long term populations must become reproductively isolated from one another if they are to maintain their integrity when conditions change. Evolution of isolating mechanisms is a crucial part of evolution. So far, specific intrinsic mechanisms which cause tolerant populations to be reproductively isolated from normal populations have not been found in the populations which have been studied (McNEILLY and ANTONOVICS, 1968). But at the other end of the evolutionary scale there do appear to be a few species which are specifically associated with metalliferous areas in southern and central Africa, such as *Dicoma niccolifera, Euphorbia wildii, Lotononis serpenticola, Pearsonia metallifera.*

Why only few and why in Africa? This is difficult to answer. The best explanation is that the evolution of distinct populations into distinct species carrying a whole range of characteristics besides metal tolerance does take a long time, and it can only occur in regions where the areas of specialized soil are large enough to allow the developing species enough variety of habitat so that they can persist through major climatic fluctuations. These large areas occur in Africa (WILD and BRADSHAW, 1977). But much more work needs to be done on this problem.

It would be a pity if all this work could only contribute to solving theoretical problems, particularly when we remember the enormous costs of pollution to agriculture and to the environment in general. Obviously we have to reduce pollution at source – this is the only sensible way. But for a long time we are going to have to face up to pollution as an inevitable part of our environment. The fact that evolution occurs in relation to pollution gives us the key of one way to combat it – by the development of new varieties with specific tolerances to pollutants. It appears that it may be no more difficult to breed varieties resistant to specific pollutants than to breed varieties adapted to specific climates and diseases, and many thousands of the latter have been produced successfully. The metal-tolerant and air pollution-tolerant material already available points the way.

Darwin in the *Origin of Species* suggested that 'evolution is silently and insensibly working at the improvement of each organic being in relation to its conditions of life'. Working in the English countryside he did not think of pollution as a contributor to evolution. One hundred years later we can see it is a potent factor with fascinating consequences.

Simple Practical Experiments

1 Effects of metals on cell division

Metals which prevent root growth can be suspected of doing so by preventing chromosome replication or cell division. So abnormalities should be found in the normal process of cell division observed in root tips.

Materials Shallots, or onion sets
Freshly prepared acetic alcohol fixative (1 glacial acetic acid: 3 absolute alcohol – coloured pale yellow with saturated solution of ferric chloride)
Aceto carmine stain
Slides, coverslips
The plants

Method The plants are rooted into deionized or distilled water which must be changed daily.

When roots are 10 mm long some of the rooted plants may be transferred to a solution containing low levels of one of the heavy metals (see Table 6).

Root tip squashes in aceto carmine stain can be made after fixing the root tips overnight in acetic alcohol. The presence or absence of cell division and the course of mitosis in treated root tips can be compared with that in control material which has not been treated.

Concentration of heavy metal and duration of the treatment at any one concentration can be varied.

2. Testing adult plants for tolerance

Tolerance to a particular metal is tested by measuring its effects on root growth. Grasses are most amenable to this type of test as they are made up of a number of genetically identical shoots or tillers which will readily root in either soil or solution. However, many other types of plants can and have been rooted successfully using this method.

Materials Plastic or polystyrene beakers (*not* glass as this tends to absorb metal ions)
Rooting solutions, one without, one with the appropriate metal level (see Table 6)

Lids to hold tillers – plastic tubes in plastic sheeting
Plant material taken when plants are not flowering or about to flower

Method Tillers possessing a basal node are carefully split off from the plant. A minimum of four tillers per treatment are needed.

The beaker and tillers should be kept in a well-lit, warm spot, under a bell jar or a box of transparent plastic sheeting to maintain humidity and prevent the tillers from drying up.

Solutions should be changed every other day to ensure aeration and to maintain metal levels.

a) The usual method is to grow samples of tillers of the material to be tested, in parallel, in:

i) control solution without metal
ii) test solution containing metal

root lengths are measured after approximately 14 days.

$$\text{Tolerance index} = \frac{\text{mean longest root length of tiller} + \text{metal}}{\text{mean longest root length of tiller} - \text{metal}} \times 100$$

b) An alternative method which requires fewer tillers uses measurements on the same tiller put first into control solution and then into test solution, in series, as follows:

i) tillers rooted as before in control solution for 7 days – length of longest root measured
ii) tillers continue growing in control solution for 3 days – increase in length of longest root measured (A)
iii) tillers continue growing in control solution containing appropriate heavy metal concentration for 3 days – increase length of longest root measured (B)

The tolerance index is now B/A × 100.

3 Testing seedlings for tolerance

Seedlings can be tested using the same metal solutions as are used for testing adult plants, except that a 1/10 strength of a normal complete nutrient solution, such as Hoaglands, the pH of which is adjusted to approximately 7.0, is used to contain the metal ions.

Materials Plastic or polystyrene beakers
Black polythene beads[1] or firm nylon mesh (nylon stocking material is excellent) to support seeds
1/10 strength nutrient solution without phosphate

---

[1] Alkathene beads Type K11/02 Black 904 obtainable from ICI Plastics Division, Welwyn Garden City, Herts.

Solution containing metal ion
Seed

Method A two layer deep raft of polythene beads is floated on the surface of the nutrient solution in the beaker without metal, or the mesh is stretched over the solution surface. Seeds are sown and will germinate on this layer.

After 7–10 days seedlings can be removed, root lengths measured, and the seedlings returned to the solution.

After a further 4 days the increase in root lengths is measured (A). The seedlings are now returned to a beaker containing nutrient solution to which has been added the appropriate level of metal (see Table 6).

After a further 4 days the increase in root length is measured (B).

The index of tolerance is calculated as B/A × 1000.

4 Screening normal populations for tolerance

Seed of normal populations of a species can be screened for the rare occurrence of tolerant individuals by growing them for some time on metal containing waste, or in metal containing solution. It is sometimes difficult to get the right sort of waste, and so it is better to use the solution technique. The rare seedlings which produce roots at a metal concentration which prevent root growth of almost every other individual will be metal tolerant. The frequency of occurrence of tolerant seedlings in different species can be compared.

Materials Black polythene beads
Washing up bowls – plastic
1/10 strength nutrient solution without phosphate
Solution containing metal ion
Seed of selected species

Method The appropriate level of metal which just prevents root growth should be determined by measuring seedling root growth in a series of concentrations of the metal, using the floating bead technique (see § 10.4).

Then using the same floating bead method in large (washing up) bowls, a very large number of seeds can be screened. Those which produce roots will be metal tolerant. This tolerance can be tested using either of the methods outlined previously for seedlings or adult plants.

5 Heritability of tolerance

The heritability of any quantitative character can be estimated from a comparison of the characteristics of a set of adult plants and their individual progenies.

Materials Collect tillers of individual adult plants together with their own inflorescences in late August/early September.

Method Grow the adult plants in potting soil. Sow a sample of seed from each adult plant on moist filter paper in a petri dish, ensuring that each adult and its seed are identifiable.

Pick out when large enough 5–10 seedlings from each parent and grow them on in potting soil.

Test the tolerance of the adults and seedlings when they are big enough to provide enough tillers for testing.

This will provide an index of tolerance value

i) for each parent

ii) for a sample of each parents' offspring.

The index of tolerance of each of the parent plants is now plotted (x axis) against the mean index of tolerance of its offspring (y axis).

The slope of this regression calculated by normal methods provides an estimate of half the narrow sense heritability of metal tolerance for the individuals sampled.

6 Evolution of herbicide resistance

It is not difficult to try selecting for herbicide resistance.

Materials A small quantity of one of the triazine group of herbicides e.g. atrazine, simazine

Garden soil sieved to pass a 6 mm mesh sieve

Seed of any common garden weed or crop plant

Seed trays

Silver sand, washed, as a carrier for the herbicide

Method Weigh sufficient simazine to give a dose rate of equivalent to 0.5 $kg\,ha^{-1}$ based on seed tray surface area. Mix thoroughly with 20 g of washed sand. Mix sand and simazine thoroughly with soil. It is crucial that this is done thoroughly. Sow seeds.

Results can be assessed after 35 days' growth. Plants that appear healthy and are actively growing with three or four true leaves may be regarded as survivors. They can then be grown on and allowed to cross with other survivors.

The seed produced should then be tested again for survival, in comparison with seed produced by other plants grown on ordinary soil.

It is easiest to choose outbreeding, variable crop plants such as rye, mustard, carrots, cabbage, radish or onion, seeds of which are easy to obtain. Do not use inbreeders such as wheat, barley or tomatoes as they possess little, if any, genetic variability.

References

ALLARD, R.W. and HANSCHE, P. E. (1964). Some parameters of population variability and their implications in plant breeding. *Adv. Agron.*, **16**, 281–325.

ANTONOVICS, J., BRADSHAW, A.D. and TURNER, R. G. (1971). Heavy metal tolerance in plants. *Adv. Ecol. Res.*, **7**, 1–85.

ASTON, J. L. and BRADSHAW, A. D. (1966). Evolution in closely adjacent plant populations. II *Agrostis stolonifera* in maritime habitats. *Heredity*, **21**, 649–64.

AYCOCK, M. K. (1972). Combining ability estimates for weather fleck in *Nicotiana tabacum* L. *Crop Science*, **12**, 672–4.

BAKER, A. J. M. (1978). Ecophysiological aspects of zinc tolerance in *Silene maritima* With. *New Phytol.*, **80**, 635–42.

BANDEEN, J. D. and McLAREN, R. D. (1976). Resistance of *Chenopodium album* L. to triazine herbicides. *Can. J. Pl. Sci.*, **56**, 411–12.

BELL, J. N. B. and MUDD, C. H. (1976). Sulphur dioxide resistance in plants: a case study of *Lolium perenne*. In *Effects of Air Pollutants on Plants*, ed. T. A. Mansfield, 87–103. Cambridge University Press, London.

BERRY, R. J. (1977). *Inheritance and Natural History*. Collins New Naturalist, **61**. Collins, Glasgow.

BRADSHAW, A. D. (1972). Some of the evolutionary consequences of being a plant. *Evol. Biol.*, **5**, 25–47.

BRADSHAW, A. D. (1976). Pollution and evolution. In *Effects of Air Pollutants on Plants*, ed. T. A. Mansfield, 135–59. Cambridge University Press, London.

BRADSHAW, A. D. and CHADWICK, M. J. (1980). *The Restoration of Land*. Blackwells, Oxford.

BRIGGS, D. and WALTERS, S. M. (1969). *Plant Variation and Evolution*. McGraw-Hill, New York.

BROKER, W. (1963). Genetisch-physiologishe Untersuchungenüber die zinkverträglichkeit von *Silene inflata* Sm. *Flora, Jena* B, **153**, 122–56.

BROWN, A. W. A. and PAL, R. (1971). Insecticide resistance in arthropods. W.H.O., Geneva.

CHARLES, A. H. (1961). Differential survival of cultivars of *Lolium, Dactylis* and *Phleum*. *J. Br. Grassl. Soc.*, **16**, 69–75.

CLAUSEN, J. (1962). *Stages in the Evolution of Plant Species*. Hafner, New York.

COOPER, J. P. (1954). Studies on growth and development in *Lolium*. IV Genetic control of heading responses in local populations. *J. Ecol.*, **42**, 521–56.

DUNN, D. B. (1959). Some effects of air pollution on *Lupinus* in the Los Angeles area. *Ecology*, **40**, 621–5.

EDWARDS, K. J. R. (1977). *Evolution in Modern Biology*, Studies in Biology no. 87. Edward Arnold, London.

FALCONER, D. S. (1960). *Introduction to Quantitative Genetics*. Oliver and Boyd, Edinburgh.

FORD, E. B. (1976). *Genetics and Adaptation*, Studies in Biology no. 69. Edward Arnold, London.

GARTSIDE, D. W. and McNEILLY, T. (1974a). Genetic studies in heavy metal tolerant plants. I Genetics of zinc tolerance in *Anthoxanthum odoratum*. *Heredity*, **32**, 287–97.

GARTSIDE, D. W. and McNEILLY, T. (1974b). The potential for evolution of heavy metal tolerance in plants II. Copper tolerance in normal populations of different plant species. *Heredity*, **32**, 335–348.

GEMMELL, R. P. (1977). *The Colonization of Industrial Waste Land*, Studies in Biology no. 80. Edward Arnold, London.

GLEAVES, J. T. (1973). Gene flow mediated by wind borne pollen. *Heredity*, **31**, 355–66.

GORHAM, E. and GORDON, A. G. (1960). Some effects of smelter pollution northeast of Falconbridge, Ontario. *Can. J. Bot.*, **38**, 307–12.

GREGORY, R. P. G. and BRADSHAW, A. D. (1965). Heavy metal tolerance in populations of *Agrostis tenuis* Sibth. and other grasses. *New Phytol.*, **64**, 131–43.

HICKEY, D. A. and McNEILLY, T. (1975). Competition between metal tolerant and normal plant populations: a field experiment on normal soil. *Evolution*, **29**, 458–64.

HOLLIDAY, R. J. and PUTWAIN, P. D. (1977). Evolution of resistance to simazine in *Senecio vulgaris* L. *Weed Res.*, **17**, 291–6.

HORSMAN, D. A., ROBERTS, T. M. and BRADSHAW, A. D. (1978). Evolution of sulphur dioxide tolerance in perennial ryegrass *Nature* 276, 493–494.

HUMPHREYS, M. O. and BRADSHAW, A. D. (1977). Genetic potential for solving problems of soil mineral stress: heavy metal toxicity. In *Plant Adaptation to Mineral Stress in Problem Soils*, ed. M. J. Wright, 95–105. Cornell University, New York.

JAIN, S. K. and BRADSHAW, A. D. (1966). Evolution in closely adjacent plant populations I. The evidence and its theoretical analysis. *Heredity*, **21**, 407–41.

KARIM, A. and BRADSHAW, A. D. (1968). Genetic variation in simazine resistance in wheat, rape and mustard. *Weed Res.*, **8**, 283–91.

LERNER, I. M. (1958). *The Genetic Basis of Selection*. Wiley, New York.

McNEILLY, T. (1968). Evolution in closely adjacent plant populations. III. *Agrostis tenuis* on a small copper mine. *Heredity*, **23**, 99–108.

McNEILLY, T. and BRADSHAW, A. D. (1968). Evolutionary processes in populations of copper tolerant *Agrostis tenuis* Sibth. *Evolution*, **22**, 108–18.

McNEILLY, T. and ANTONOVICS, J. A. (1968). Evolution in closely adjacent plant populations. IV. Barriers to gene flow. *Heredity*, **23**, 205–18.

MARRIAGE, P. B. and WARWICK, S. I. (1980). Differential growth and response to atrazine between and within susceptible and resistant biotypes of *Chenopodium album* L. *Weed Res.*, **20**, 9–15.

MATHER, K. and JINKS, J. L. (1976). *Introduction to Biometrical Genetics*. Chapman & Hall, London.

MATHYS, W. (1977). The role of malate, oxalate, and mustard oil glucosides in the evolution of zinc resistance in herbage. *Physiol. Plant.*, **40**, 130–6.

MELLANBY, K. (1980). *The Biology of Pollution*, 2nd edition, Studies in Biology no. 38. Edward Arnold, London.

MENSER, H. A. and HODGES, T. K. (1952). Oxidant injury to shade tobacco cultivars developed in Connecticut for weather fleck resistance. *Agron. J.*, **64**, 189–92.

PRAT, S. (1934). Die Erblichkeit der Resistenz gegen Kupfer. *Ber. Dt. Bot. Ges.*, **102**, 65–7.

ROBERTSON, F. W. (1955). Selection response and the properties of genetic variation. *Cold Spr. Harb. Symp. Quant. Biol.*, **20**, 166–7.

RUSSELL, G. and MORRIS, D. P. (1970). Copper tolerance in the marine fouling alga, *Ectocarpus siliculosus. Nature*, **228**, 288–9.

RYAN, G. F. (1970). Resistance of common groundsel to simazine and atrazine. *Weed Sci.*, **18**, 614–16.

RYDER, E. J. (1973). Selecting and breeding plants for increased resistance to air pollutants. In *Air Pollution Damage to Vegetation*, ed. J. A. Naegele, Advances in Chemistry Series 122, 75–84. American Chemical Society, Washington, D. C.

SIMON, E. (1977). Cadmium tolerance in populations of *Agrostis tenuis* and *Festuca ovina. Nature*, **265**, 329–30.

SMITH, R. A. H. and BRADSHAW, A. D. (1972). Stabilization of toxic mine wastes by the use of tolerant plant populations. *Trans. Inst. Min. Metall.*, **81** A, 230–7.

SMITH, R. A. H. and BRADSHAW, A. D. (1979). The use of metal tolerant plant populations for the reclamation of metalliferous wastes. *J. Appl. Ecol.*, **16**, 595–612.

SNAYDON, R. W. (1970). Rapid population differentiation in a mosaic environment. I. The response of *Anthoxanthum odoratum* populations to soils. *Evolution*, **24**, 257–69.

SNAYDON, R. W. and BRADSHAW, A. D. (1961). Differential response to calcium within the species *Festuca ovina* L. *New Phytol.*, **60**, 219–34.

SNAYDON, R. W. and DAVIES, M. S. (1976). Rapid population differentiation in a mosaic environment. IV. Populations of *Anthoxanthum odoratum* at sharp boundaries. *Heredity*, **37**, 9–25.

TAYLOR, G. E. (1978). Genetic analysis of ecotypic differentiation of an annual plant species, *Geranium carolinianum* L., in response to sulfur dioxide. *Bot. Gaz.*, **139**, 362–8.

TAYLOR, G. E. and MURDY, W. H. (1975). Population differentiation of an annual plant species, *Geranium carolinianum* L., in response to sulfur dioxide. *Bot. gaz.*, **136**, 212–15.

TURNER, R. G. and MARSHALL, C. (1972). Accumulation of zinc by subcellular fractions of roots of *A. tenuis* Sibth. in relation to zinc tolerance. *New Phytol.*, **71**, 671–6.

WALLEY, K. A., KHAN, M. S. I. and BRADSHAW, A. D. (1974). The potential for evolution of heavy metal tolerance in plants. I. Copper and zinc tolerance in *Agrostis tenuis. Heredity*, **32**, 309–19.

WILD, H. and BRADSHAW, A. D. (1977). The evolutionary effects of metalliferous and other anomalous soils in S. Central Africa. *Evolution*, **31**, 282–93.

WU, L., BRADSHAW, A. D. and THURMAN, D. A. (1975). The potential for evolution of heavy metal tolerance in plants. III. The rapid evolution of copper tolerance in *Agrostis stolonifera. Heredity*, **34**, 165–87.

WOODWORTH, C. M., LENG, E. R. and JUGENHEIMER, R. W. (1952). Fifty generations of selection for protein and soil in corn. *Agron. J.*, **44**, 60–6.

WU, L., THURMAN, D. A. and BRADSHAW, A. D. (1975). The uptake of copper and its effect on respiratory processes of roots of copper-tolerant and non-tolerant clones of *Agrostis stolonifera. New Phytol.*, **75**, 225–9.